*To my wonderful wife, Donna*

*Thanks for all of the
writing-the-book dates*

Until one is committed, there is hesitancy, the chance to draw back, always ineffectiveness. Concerning all acts of initiative and creation, there is one elementary truth the ignorance of which kills countless ideas and splendid plans: that the moment one definitely commits oneself, then providence moves too.

All sorts of things occur to help one that would never have otherwise occurred. A whole stream of events issues from the decision, raising in one's favor all manner of unforeseen incidents and meetings and material assistance, which no man could have dreamed would have come his way.

Whatever you can do or dream you can, begin it. Boldness has genius, power and magic in it. Begin it now.

*Goethe*

# PERSONALITY SELLING

## Selling the Way Customers Want to Buy

## TOM ANASTASI

Sterling Publishing Co., Inc.   New York

Edited by Claire Bazinet

**Library of Congress Cataloging-in-Publication Data**

Anastasi, Thomas E.
    Personality selling : selling the way customers want to buy / by Tom Anastasi.
       p.     cm.
    Includes bibliographical references and index.
    ISBN 0-8069-8536-4
    1. Selling—Psychological aspects.  2. Personality.  I. Title.
HF5438.8.P75A5    1992
658.8'5—dc20                                 91-47081
                                                  CIP

10  9  8  7  6  5  4  3  2  1

Published in 1992 by Sterling Publishing Company, Inc.
387 Park Avenue South, New York, N.Y. 10016
© 1992 by Tom Anastasi
Distributed in Canada by Sterling Publishing
% Canadian Manda Group, P.O. Box 920, Station U
Toronto, Ontario, Canada M8Z 5P9
Distributed in Great Britain and Europe by Cassell PLC
Villiers House, 41/47 Strand, London WC2N 5JE, England
Distributed in Australia by Capricorn Link Ltd.
P.O. Box 665, Lane Cove, NSW 2066
*Manufactured in the United States of America*
*All rights reserved*

Sterling ISBN 0-8069-8536-4

# CONTENTS

# PREFACE

Why Personality Selling (TM)?[1] I developed the idea of Personality Selling because I could see that it was desperately needed. I realized this when, as a salesman, I took several kinds of training courses that did little to help me get more and bigger sales, much to annoy me.

The courses didn't help me much, because the instructors all tried to teach me to sell the way they did, and the way they sold wasn't right for me. I couldn't sustain it. The courses also annoyed me because I always had the feeling that the instructors thought I was broken, and it was up to them to fix me. I've since found that my feelings are shared by thousands of salespeople who each year read books on sales or take courses that try to "fix them." I don't need fixing!

Personality Selling doesn't try to mold you into someone you're not. Instead, in the chapters ahead, you'll discover what aspects of your personality make you the kind of salesperson you are. You'll also learn how to adapt the way you sell to the way your customers want to buy. You'll be surprised to learn why your customers behave the way they do. Instead of trying to make you into a carbon copy of the author, *Personality Selling* will give you the key to becoming the best version of who you are.

The personality theory of Personality Selling is combined with a proven selling framework that you can use with all types of customers in all sales situations. Experienced salespeople can adapt the framework to the way they already sell. New salespeople can use it to develop sales procedures that will bring them success right from the start. This is because new salespeople will have learned, by the end of this book, what many salespeople spent years learning, on the road.

Whether you're an experienced sales rep, a novice salesperson, or haven't actually started selling yet, *Personality Selling* will help you understand how your customers think, close more sales, and make more money.

Enjoy *Personality Selling*. Good luck and good selling!

Tom Anastasi

# ACKNOWLEDGMENTS

The biggest thanks for this book go to the hundreds of customers I have had over the years. You paid my mortgage and put food on my table. You, knowingly and unknowingly, were the proving ground for Personality Selling. I appreciate every sale.

Before getting started with Personality Selling, I'd like to thank the people who helped me bring it to you. These people did everything from editorial consulting to personality consulting. They are Jim and Michelle Irvine, Harry Huggins, Marta Certa, Don Mitchell, Tom O'Leary, and Rife Boston.

Special thanks, of course, go to my parents, Tom and Dorothy Anastasi, for having me; my sisters, Nancy Anastasi and Catherine Anastasi Van, for providing the appropriate amount of sisterly criticism, encouragement, and advice on commas; my brother-in-law, Glenn Van, noted theologian and sales expert, for his pearls that hopefully were not trampled; and especially to my wife, Donna, for, among many other things, making sure that Introverts, Feeling types, and Perceiving types got their day in court.

I'd also like to thank Robert Benfari, Ph.D., of Harvard University's School of Public Health, a leading expert in organization behavior, for first introducing me to the field of organization psychology and for encouraging me to take an idea and run with it.

Finally, I'd like to thank all the Sterling team, especially Charles Nurnberg and my editor, Claire Bazinet, for getting this book out to you.

# PART I
# How Personality Selling Works

# Chapter 1
# PERSONALITY SELLING =
# SUCCESSFUL SELLING

Conventional wisdom says that business is "buying things and selling them for more." Personality Selling, the marriage of sales skills and psychology, picks up where conventional wisdom leaves off by showing you *how* to put yourself in the picture and sell those products, services, etc., for more. It's a behavioral approach to selling that enables you to make the most of your natural sales ability and better understand your customers' buying behavior. You do this by discovering and keying-in on your and your customers' personality traits. Once you recognize these traits, and understand their influence on behavior in the market-place, you can adapt your natural sales methods to individual customers' buying styles.

Do you often wonder why some customers are so much easier to sell to than others? The reason is simple. People with personality traits similar to yours see things as you do, so your styles merge. Your way of selling complements their way of buying. Communication flows easily. On the other hand, people who don't share your personality traits, or have opposing ones, see things differently so that you have to work harder to get your message across. Through Personality Selling, how-ever, you can determine a customer's preferences and modify your approach accordingly. Suddenly, your selling style "clicks" with their buying style. Everyone becomes an easy-to-sell-to customer. (Except, of course, for the "difficult" ones. We'll tackle them in chapter 10.)

## Personality Selling Is Like Baseball

Think, for a moment, of professional baseball. When salespeople use Personality Selling, they adapt their sales styles to customers the way professional baseball players (the good ones) adapt their hitting styles to each individual pitcher. Hank Aaron used the same batting techniques throughout his career, but got the hits, and home runs, because he adapted his swing to many different pitching styles. Sometimes he swung aggressively. Other times he waited calmly and confidently for a certain pitch. Each time he stood in the batter's box, he made slight adjustments in his style designed to maximize his potential against that guy on the mound.

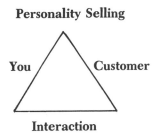

**Personality Selling**

You — Customer

**Interaction**

Likewise, salespeople who Personality Sell change their selling styles based on the preferences of different customers. For instance, sometimes you'll need to prepare a detailed, high-tech extravaganza for fifty people to get the sale. Other times you'll need to have a quiet, no-frills, one-on-one conversation. Sales reps have long relied on intuition or guesswork to "sell" customers, some salespeople more successfully than others. Now, using the techniques in *Personality Selling*, you can adapt the way you sell to all types of customers in all types of sales situations from retail to high finance. There's no stopping you.

# The Four Areas (or Indexes) of Personality Selling

Personality Selling is based on indexes of four behavioral areas which predict how people react to people; for our purposes, how customers react to salespeople and how salespeople deal with customers. These predictive traits, combined with sales skills, tell you exactly how to sell to anyone.

All four indexes are covered in detail in the chapters ahead, along with practical, step-by-step information on how to use Personality Selling to analyze and respond correctly to common, everyday sales situations.

Here's a selection of circumstances you might encounter and questions Personality Selling will help you answer.

> **SITUATION:** You're planning to meet a customer next week to deliver a proposal.
> **QUESTION:** Should you send your proposal to the customer before the meeting or not? (The answer is covered in chapter 2.)

**SITUATION:** A customer asks you for evidence to support the claim that your product is superior.
**QUESTION:** Should your supporting data be presented as a spreadsheet or a graph? (The answer is covered in chapter 3.)

**SITUATION:** You're presenting your product's benefits.
**QUESTION:** Should you emphasize that your product cuts production costs, or that it increases employee job satisfaction? (The answer is covered in chapter 4.)

**SITUATION:** You've just finished your presentation.
**QUESTION:** Should you ask for the order right away, or wait? (The answer is covered in chapter 5.)

Salespeople dealing in all types of products and services face these tough sales decisions every day. The most effective strategies to use depend on the customer. Doing what's instinctive for you, only works with customers who think as you do. You may have won some sales because your competitor sold the wrong way and "turned-off" the sale, while you just happened to sell according to the customer's buying preferences. With Personality Selling, you will understand why you won those sales and learn how you can get lots more.

# Jungian Theory and the Art of Personality Selling

Personality Selling uses personality theory to predict a customer's behavior accurately. It is based on Carl Jung's work on personality type.[2] Jungian personality type is measured in many ways, the two most common being the Kiersey & Bates temperament sorter and the Myers-Briggs Type Indicator (MBTI),®[3] which is widely used today as a management development tool. Two psychologists, Isabell Myers and Katherine Briggs, developed the MBTI to help people understand each other better. It has now been used in business for over forty years, and has been validated in hundreds of scientific studies. Thousands of companies, including Apple Computer, ITT, and Digital Equipment Corporation, administered the MBTI half a million times last year.[4]

Many salespeople have never heard about Jungian type theory or how the MBTI measures preferences, so they are unaware of their value in sales. Based on the same indexes used in the MBTI, Personality Selling describes and categorizes behavior four ways, with each category, or index, offering two alternative tendencies, for a total of eight separate behavioral traits or preferences.

# The Eight Preferences

Here is a brief overview of the eight preferences or functions and their individual importance to salespeople. The preferences will be covered in detail and in combinations in the chapters ahead, with helpful examples of their usefulness in selling.

## Index #1 Introvert/Extrovert

The Introvert/Extrovert index is useful when prospecting for new accounts, or communicating with customers.

**INTROVERT:** Introverts like to analyze information alone and don't like unexpected calls or visits.
**IMPORTANCE TO SALESPEOPLE:** Make sure you contact Introverts when you won't be a distraction. Put it in writing, or ask for a good time to speak with them.

**EXTROVERT:** Extroverts like being part of a group and discussing options and possibilities with salespeople.
**IMPORTANCE TO SALESPEOPLE:** Meet with Extroverted customers regularly, and spend time going over your proposals with them.

## Index #2 Sensing/Intuitive

The Sensing/Intuitive index is especially useful when deciding the content of customer presentations.

**SENSING:** Sensing types like a lot of data and want solutions to have practical benefit. They'll notice every detail.
**IMPORTANCE TO SALESPEOPLE:** Prepare a conservative, logical and flawless proposal rich in detail.

**INTUITIVE:** Intuitives like discussing ideas and possibilities, rather than factual data.
**IMPORTANCE TO SALESPEOPLE:** Presentations to Intuitives should be an overview, rich in theory but with a minimum of detail.

## Index #3 Thinking/Feeling

The Thinking/Feeling index comes into play when handling objections. It alerts you to what type of objections to expect and the best way to handle them.

**THINKING:** Thinking types make decisions objectively and analytically.

**IMPORTANCE TO SALESPEOPLE:** Stress the logical reasons for their buying what you sell.

**FEELING:** Feeling types make decisions based on improving the quality of people's lives.
**IMPORTANCE TO SALESPEOPLE:** Stress the human benefits of what you sell.

## Index #4 Judging/Perceiving

The Judging/Perceiving index is the key indicator for knowing when and how to close a sale because it measures a person's view of time in decision making.

**JUDGING:** Judging types like making schedules and deadlines and keeping to them.
**IMPORTANCE TO SALESPEOPLE:** When selling to a Judging type, make sure you keep to their buying schedule.

**PERCEIVING:** Perceiving types like flexible schedules and deadlines and are careful decision makers.
**IMPORTANCE TO SALESPEOPLE:** Be flexible with the Perceiving types. If a timely buying decision needs to be made, explain why and help them set up a schedule.

# MBTI Shorthand

The MBTI uses a preference's first letter as abbreviation for that trait, as follows:

| Index 1 | | Index 2 | | Index 3 | | Index 4 | |
|---|---|---|---|---|---|---|---|
| E | Extrovert | S | Sensing | T | Thinking | J | Judging |
| I | Introvert | N | Intuitive | F | Feeling | P | Perceiving |

Note: You can't use I for Intuitive in the second index because it's taken up by Introvert in the first index.

According to MBTI theory, each of us leans toward one or the other trait in each of the four behavioral areas or indexes. The four index preferences, collectively, make up our personality type. There are therefore sixteen possible personality types. (One, for example, is Extrovert, Sensing, Thinking, Judging or ESTJ type.) No wonder a salesperson needs to Personality Sell to consistently make the sale.

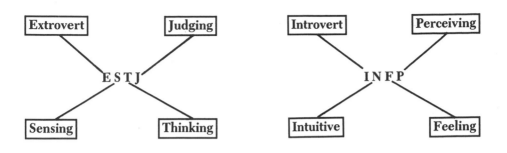

# People Are Unaware of Their Preferences

Most of us are largely unaware that we have the kind of biases listed above, although we all do. Extroverts, for instance, tend to relax by going to a crowded city where they can interact freely, while Introverts tend to relax by going to a secluded lake where they can be alone. Making an Introvert shop at malls during the holiday season or an Extrovert spend the weekend in retreat at a monastery is like making left-handed people write with their right hands. They can do it, but it won't be natural or easy.

# Customers Buy the "Easy" Way

These preferences determine a customer's "buying biases." People buy the way that's most comfortable for them, and they seek reps who will conform to and reinforce their buying biases. They'll give their business to the salesperson who makes buying easy, even enjoyable, for them. For every customer, Personality Selling will ensure that you'll be one of those salespeople who make buying easy.

# When Selling Loses Sales

Selling against a customer's buying biases can hurt even conscientious, good-intentioned reps. Sometimes salespeople sell the way they, themselves, would want to be sold to instead of the way the individual customer wants to buy. Unfortunately, situations like the following happen every day to diligent salespeople who don't know about Personality Selling:

Jane, a computer store rep, knew her customer, Jerry, had several meetings every day. Meetings tired her. She assumed Jerry felt the same, so Jane always called Jerry with information and took his orders over the phone.

What Jane didn't know is that Jerry liked meetings, and found talking to people on the phone tedious. After changing vendors, he explained, "Jane was conscientious, but I never saw her, and I don't want to buy from a voice on the phone."

If Jane had known about Personality Selling, she would have asked Jerry whether he preferred meetings or phone calls. She then would have ignored her own preference, met with him periodically, and wouldn't have lost the account.

Jerry wasn't being mean or callous. Like most customers, he didn't realize he had such strong personal biases, so Jerry couldn't tell Jane how to sell to him. Customers usually feel bad about cutting off salespeople they know work hard for them, but they are always looking for people who sell the way they want to buy.

## Trained Buyers Will Tell You

Unlike selling to the typical consumer, selling to trained buyers is easy because they realize they're particular about how they want to be sold to. They eliminate guesswork by telling you flat out what their biases are:

> "I want a quote listing prices and part numbers on Wednesday, so we can review it Friday afternoon. Also, I don't like phone calls in the morning."

Any salesperson worth his salt would respond exactly the way this buyer wants. He'd have the quotation ready Wednesday and would not pick up the phone until after lunch. Unfortunately, most customers aren't trained buyers and don't make their sales rep's job that easy.

## Customers Don't Tell You How to Sell Them

Most customers, in fact, won't verbalize their personality traits at all, so it's up to you, using Personality Selling, to discover how they want to be approached. An important part of Personality Selling is identifying your customers' buying biases by asking the right questions and making the right observations. You'll want to know: 1) how customers want to receive information from you, 2) what supporting information and how many details are best to give, 3) which people buy because of analytical reasoning and which buy based on emotion, and 4) when customers will buy, and how much you can push them.

After you know who wants what, and give it to them, selling to anyone will be easy. You'll be selling the way they want to buy.

# How Experienced Salespeople Sell

Over their careers many experienced salespeople have learned on their own to adapt their styles in response to customers' buying biases: Personality Selling without knowing it. After meeting with countless customers over a number of years, they have gained such experience by having learned from every sale they won or lost. Experience teaches salespeople, for instance, which customers like to get right down to business, and which like to chat for a while first. Through *Personality Selling* you'll know what salespeople have had to learn by experience. The difference is that you'll know, by the end of this book, what it used to take ten to fifteen years or more for salespeople to pick up on the streets. When people learn Personality Selling techniques through experience, they often don't know what components make it up, so they can't tell you *how* they do it. This book can.

Using a combination of your natural sales abilities and Personality Selling, you'll sell effectively to customers with personalities similar to yours and, more to the point, with biases different from yours. Even the "tough prospects" your predecessors have had trouble with will be easy for you to figure out.

# Conclusion

Personality Selling helps you gain maximum sales by showing you how to adapt your personal sales approach to the customer and situation at hand. Many salespeople feel the best part of Personality Selling is that they can just be themselves. They don't have to say or do things that make them feel uncomfortable or foolish. Personality Selling doesn't try to make you copy other successful salespeople, because "power salesmanship" can't be canned. Instead of trying to "fix" you or turn you into something you're not, Personality Selling gives you the tools to be the best version of who you are. You outsell your competitors by discovering your customers' buying biases and selling to them the way they want to buy, the way a professional baseball player adapts his batting style to different pitchers. The end result is that each customer contact will be all that it can be.

# Know Yourself

If you want to know now what your personality type is, complete The Sales Personality Guide, Appendix A. This is not the Myers-Briggs Type Indicator. Based on the answers that salespeople and managers gave in Sales and Negotiation Training Company seminars, the Sales Personality Guide will, however, give you a working knowledge of your psychological preferences.

If you would rather learn your personality type along with information about what it all means to you, continue reading. The Sales Personality Guide questions relating to the four behavioral indexes are included in chapters 2 through 5.

# PART II
# A Complete Sales Cycle the Personality Selling Way

# Chapter 2
# COLD CONTACTING—MORE CUSTOMERS THAN YOU CAN HANDLE

Depending on his or her personality type, every customer has a preferred way of being contacted by salespeople. Some people like crowded malls where vendors show and ask them to buy things, while others prefer choosing what they want from the Home Shopping Network or mail order catalogs.

Some people want personal visits from salespeople, while others want phone calls, and still others want letters that they can read privately. The challenge salespeople face is deciding which approach to use with a specific customer—especially since the wrong type of contact will probably be unsuccessful. Extroverts will likely throw away sales letters and Introverts will refuse unexpected visits or phone calls.

With Personality Selling you'll know beforehand the best method of contacting prospective accounts. Each cold-contact will be successful and start the sales process.

## Sales Calls Are Cheap ... Or Expensive

Sales calls can be either cheap or expensive, for both you and your company, depending on the outcome. Many reports peg the cost of sales calls at $300 to $500 each. The expensive calls are the ones that you go on that don't bring in any business. The cheap ones are the calls that bring in much more than the $300 they cost.

Most sales calls pay for themselves many times over, or companies wouldn't need salespeople, just catalogs. The problem salespeople face is that they don't know, before the fact, which call is going to be one of the cheap ones or one of the expensive ones.

Although you can't know for sure, before the call, if it's going to be a gusher, you can increase your chances for success by finding likely prospects, choosing the best cold-contacting method for each customer, and qualifying your prospects. Then use Personality Selling, and your natural talent, to get the big accounts you deserve.

# Find the Prospects

Who are the prime prospects? Where are they? Whom should I contact? These are common questions salespeople ask. It's difficult to find this type of information in the phone book, or through asking other customers or friends. You'll find all the big accounts you can handle by visiting the business and reference sections of your library. References like the *Standard & Poor's Register of Corporations, Directors and Executives* (Vol. 3) and Dun & Bradstreet investment guides, which give company ratings, will tell you who and where the accounts in your territory are. These and other such guides often list companies by state, with several ways of listing companies within each state. They list the 1000 companies with the most employees, the 1000 with the most revenue, and the 1000 with the most profits. They also list corporations alphabetically and by industry, following the Standard Industrial Classification (SIC) code set up by the Federal government. For example, you'll find all the transportation companies, all the office supply companies, or all the clothing manufacturers grouped together. There are SIC codes for industries you might not even realize exist. If you're selling to a vertical or a specialized market, this can be a real time-saver. All you have to do is look up the SIC code of the vertical you're interested in and you'll find all the prospects listed together in categories, courtesy of Uncle Sam. You'll have the addresses, phone numbers, and company contacts of as many leads as you can handle. Check around, too, for other business reference books like *The National Directory, Moody's Guide to Publicly Held Companies*, Statistical Abstracts, and *Facts on File* publications.

After you've exhausted all the sources in the library, check your local chamber of commerce, state government agencies, the Yellow Pages, the Help Wanted section of the newspaper, and the Business to Business Pages. Finally, keep your eyes open as you make your rounds so you don't drive past business opportunities without stopping.

# What Is It You Sell—Are You Sure?

Before contacting anyone, you have to know what it is you sell. Do you know what you sell? Many reps don't. Let's see what Forge sells:

> At a Forge Hardware meeting the sales manager asked the reps to tell him what the store sells. One rep eagerly volunteered, "We sell drills, sir."
>
> "No, we don't. I've worked for Forge for twenty years and never sold a drill."

"But sir, I sold a drill yesterday."

"No, you didn't. Nobody needs drills. What people need are holes. A drill is just one way of getting the hole. If you're selling drills, you're selling the wrong thing. What we're selling here are holes."

People don't need computers, they need to be able to track their accounts receivable. They don't need insurance, they need protection against financially disastrous events.

Sell holes, not drills.

# The First Contact: In Person, Phone Call, or Letter?

After returning from the library armed with leads, you'll need to contact the prospective accounts. The way you make the initial or cold contact depends on your own personality preferences and on the prospect's probable biases. The three main ways to cold-contact customers are in person, by phone (also known as telemarketing), and through mailings. Each has its pluses and minuses.

Of the four behavioral areas involved in Personality Selling, the most important for cold-contacting prospective customers is the Introvert/Extrovert index. This is the index that lets you know which cold-contacting method would be best to use, so let's look at it now.

# The Introvert/Extrovert Index

The Introvert/Extrovert index is the key to learning how people prefer to interact with others, including salespeople. Introverts and Extroverts want to be contacted, met with, and dealt with in completely opposite ways. Choosing the right way will make your job easier. Choosing the wrong way could make your job impossible, or at best more difficult because the contact will be met with little enthusiasm.

Introverts and Extroverts find being alone a very different experience. Introverts do their best thinking when alone. They're invigorated when they're working in their offices with the door closed. Extroverts, on the other hand, do their best thinking in meetings where they can share and develop ideas with others. Extroverts find being in a crowded, noisy lunchroom or working from an open office with several desks nearby (known as the bull pen) energizing. They find being alone, isolated from others, draining.

The vast majority, over 75 percent, of salespeople are Extroverts.[5] Most managers, on the other hand, are Introverts.[6] Which type are you? If you're not sure and want to find out, complete the following portion of the Personality Selling Guide or the complete exercise in Appendix A.

**DIRECTIONS:** Read each of these ten items and circle either answer A or B, depending on which response fits you best. There are no right, wrong, or better answers. You'll find the key to scoring at the end of this series of questions.

1. **If someone asks you a question, do you usually:**
   A) reflect for a few moments, then respond.
   B) respond quickly.
2. **You like:**
   A) short meetings.
   B) long meetings.
3. **Would you rather have meetings:**
   A) with one person.
   B) with a group of people.
4. **If a customer wants you to get back to them, would you prefer:**
   A) writing a proposal and sending it to them.
   B) meeting with them and talking about it.
5. **Do you prefer being with people who are:**
   A) somewhat quiet.
   B) talkative.
6. **Would you rather have a:**
   A) desk in an open area.
   B) private office.
7. **Do you find your most tiring days to be:**
   A) days when there are a lot of meetings.
   B) days when you are alone.
8. **If there is a long period of silence during a conversation, is it your inclination to:**
   A) fill it in.
   B) use it to think.
9. **Would you prefer:**
   A) introducing yourself to someone.
   B) having someone introduce you.
10. **When thinking over a new idea, do you prefer:**
    A) taking a walk someplace quiet, alone.
    B) talking it out with colleagues.

**SCORING:**
Add the **A** answers for questions
1, 2, 3, 4, 5
Add the **B** answers for questions
6, 7, 8, 9, 10

Put the Total here:_____ I/E

If the Total is 5 or more you're most likely an **Introvert**. Otherwise, you're most likely an **Extrovert**.

## Occupations Common to Introverts and Extroverts

Because of their preferences, Introverts and Extroverts have tended to gravitate toward certain career areas. Following are lists of occupations where Introverts and Extroverts predominate.[7] They are ranked according to percentage. (It should be remembered that, while one or the other predominates, there will always be a mix of both types; i.e., every sales rep won't be an Extrovert or every banker an Introvert. Try to confirm a customer's preferences before initiating, or early-on in, the cold-contact.)

| Introverts Predominate | Extroverts Predominate |
| --- | --- |
| manager | salesperson |
| banker | marketer |
| engineer | police officer |
| accountant | construction worker |
| farmer | receptionist |
| mechanic | waiter/waitress |
| programmer | teacher |
| surveyor | nurse |
| psychiatrist | office manager |
| social worker | cleric |
| researcher | lawyer |
| photographer | politician |

As you can see from the lists, Introverts prefer occupations and professions where they can be alone and think by themselves. They prefer a moderate to low amount of human interaction. Extroverts prefer professions that allow them to talk with others regularly and frequently, which is why so many Extroverts are associated with the sales and marketing fields.

Although there are many less of them, Introverted salespeople are effective, too. Often Introverted salespeople develop long and lasting associations with Introverted customers, who appreciate not being overwhelmed by the Extroverted reps who aren't Personality Selling. Introverted salespeople are often just as good as their Extroverted counterparts at the fundamentals of the job, like meetings and in-person cold-contacting. These activities are just harder and come less naturally to them.

## Meeting with Introverts

The best time to meet with Introverts is after they have had a chance to be by themselves for a while, because human contact and conversation tend to be exhausting for them. You'll have better luck selling to Introverts when they're fresh and alert. Although everyone's schedule is different, the best times to meet with Introverts are usually the first thing in the morning, around lunch time, or at the end of the day. The meetings should be kept short, with as few involved as needed. Introverts prefer to keep meetings to a minimum, so they'll want a scheduled meeting instead of an impromptu one. At the meeting, Introverts will want to get down to business quickly and won't want to chat for very long.

## Meeting with Extroverts

Extroverted customers enjoy meetings, so any time their schedule allows will be good for them to get together. Large meetings with much discussion tend to be better for Extroverts. To begin, they'll usually want to talk about nonbusiness-related subjects for a while, especially if they've been by themselves in the office for a good bit of time beforehand. Being alone is wearing to Extroverts. They need social interaction to "charge their batteries"[8] before they can start talking business.

## Typing Your Customer

You can find out where your customer is on the Introvert/Extrovert scale by listening and observing. No one is purely an Introvert or Extrovert, but everyone has a bias. Your customers' preference is their most comfortable way of dealing with people, and the thought processes that usually work best for them, given a choice. Still, there will be times when an Extrovert will choose to be alone and when an Introvert will want to discuss a problem with several people.

Jungian psychologists say that everyone has a single preference within each behavioral index. For the purposes of Personality Selling, you can discover your customer's Introvert/Extrovert preference by asking these types of questions:

> **SALES REP:** I have a solution for you. We could discuss it now or I could put the information in report form and you could get back to me on it. Which would you prefer?

(Extroverts will want to discuss the solution. Introverts will prefer to look it over and reflect on it first.)

> **SALES REP:** Would you like me to call you with the answer or fax it to you?

(Extroverts will prefer the phone call. Introverts will prefer the fax.)

## Personality Selling to Introverts and Extroverts

When Personality Selling, remember that Extroverts like to discuss information and like frequent, large group meetings. Introverts like to review information by themselves and like to have small, infrequent meetings. Adjust the way you sell to the way customers want to buy.

Throughout the rest of the book there will be examples of how best to apply this information on selling to Introverts and Extroverts in a variety of sales situations.

Now that you know about Introverts and Extroverts, let's look at how to contact them.

## Making the First Contact

Now that you know your own Introvert/Extrovert type and how to discover your customer's probable personality type (through the occupational listing above and other investigation), use one or a combination of the cold-contacting strategies below to bring in prospects. If you're an experienced cold-contacter, go ahead and contact your best prospects immediately, spending time with those customers with the biggest potential. If you're an inexperienced cold-contacter, begin by approaching some smaller, likely customers first. That way you'll get your feet wet and be going after the bigger and better prospects as your technique improves.

## In-Person Calls

The first method we'll look at is the in-person cold contact. These are the calls salespeople make when they personally show up unannounced to sell to customers.

**PLUSES:** In-person calls are definitely best for Extroverted reps and customers. Extroverts like interacting with people, and in-person calls are easy for them. Your message has impact when you're in front of the customer because they can really see your enthusiasm for the product and perhaps look over a sample. During the meeting, too, you can use all your powers of observation to pick up on the customer's verbal and nonverbal clues. Finally, you can get a feeling for the office and their needs and see if they're using your competitor's products.

**MINUSES:** Cold calling in person won't work well with Introverted customers. They'll see an unexpected call as an interruption. Introverted salespeople find large doses of human contact draining and may want to schedule only a few calls a day. Driving from prospect to prospect makes in-person cold calls time consuming if the territory is spread out. Most cold calls tend to be wasted on unqualified prospects and are unsuccessful. You can dial faster than you can drive.

**KEYS FOR SUCCESS:** Avoid in-person cold calling in industries that you know have a high percentage of Introverts. If you're an Introvert, remember that in-person cold calling will be tiring for you, so do it in short spurts and schedule quiet, reflective periods to enervate yourself.

When cold calling, put customers at east. Many people are anxious about "being sold to," so don't "sell to them." Tell the prospective customers you don't want to sell them anything. You just want to introduce yourself and let them know who you are, and what you do. If they can't see you when you call, you may want to tell them that you're "going to be in the area again soon" (even if you're not) so they don't feel pressured by your having to make a special trip to accommodate them. Anything you can do to put customers at ease prevents them from building a psychological wall between you that hinders listening. Try this:

> **SALESPERSON:** Hi. My name's Phil Mosier. I'm the rep in this area for Harper's office products. We sell fireproof filing systems. I don't want to sell you anything today but, if I dropped off some literature, would you have time to look at it?

**PROSPECT:** I'm busy right now, but we do need some protection for the files. Could you come by next week and tell me all about your products?
**SALESPERSON:** Sure.

## Telemarketing

Telemarketing cold contacts are similar to in-person cold contacts but, instead of visiting the prospect, you phone them.

PLUSES: Introverted salespeople prefer doing telemarketing over in-person cold-contacting because they can do it from a controlled, quiet, and private environment. Extroverted customers like getting unexpected calls from salespeople because they like talking to people and it breaks up the day.

Unqualified customers can be weeded out quickly when you let your fingers do the walking. Telemarketing is a good way to offer well-known or inexpensive products but, under most circumstances, people won't buy things sight unseen. Telemarketing, however, is a perfect vehicle for setting up meetings.

MINUSES: Many people are annoyed by unsolicited phone calls. Introverted customers despise being interrupted by someone they do not know. For these people, telemarketing will have limited positive impact. Extroverted salespeople will find telemarketing tiring because of the limited face-to-face contact. Some Introverts won't like telemarketing because they'll quickly become tired of "all the talking." Telemarketing is not good for selling expensive or unknown items because customers will want to see and examine such things before making any decision to buy.

KEYS FOR SUCCESS: Think of telemarketing as if it were a movie preview. Give prospects the highlights, the stars, a thrilling scene that will entice them into wanting to see the "whole show" so they'll have reasons to schedule a meeting. Again, say you'll be in the area and you want to introduce yourself. Tell the prospect you'd just like five minutes of his or her time—this keeps them comfortable and increases your chances of getting the meeting. If you're doing consumer, at-home, telemarketing, expect that a fair share of the people you call will not appreciate it. Anything beyond "No, thank you" on their part, however, isn't necessary and their rudeness is their problem, not yours.

There's a good amount of repetition in telemarketing. When what you say bores you, remember that the people you're calling are hearing it for the first time and are often very interested in what you're saying. Zero Mostel performed the role of Tevye in *Fiddler on the Roof* thousands of times, but each performance seemed to have the enthusiasm of the first. If motivation is tough, try to vary what you say and the way you say it.

## Letters

The third type of cold-contacting is by mail: sending something, usually an introductory letter and some product information, to a prospect to read.

**PLUSES:** A good mail-merged list, printed with a laser printer, can churn out thousands of letters a day. Cold-contact letters cost about $2.00 each and pull response rates of two to three percent ($30 to $50 per response.)[9] Customers can read letters at their convenience, so long or short letters are equally effective. Cold-contacting by letter is the best, perhaps the only, way to reach many customers. Introverts who would screen out phone calls and visits, might read letters and other materials and contact *you* if they want more information.

Contact and address lists can be bought somewhat inexpensively. These lists can have very broad or very narrow demographics targeting so you can mass mail to a niche market easily.

**MINUSES:** People associate cold letters with junk mail. Your message will be thrown out more often than read, especially by Extroverts, who tend to find reading letters dull and tiring. Other people will read the letter with interest, but will procrastinate or won't overcome inertia and respond.

**KEYS FOR SUCCESS:** Write your letter similar to an ad. Include a clever headline, snappy copy, and a picture, if possible. People will look at cold letters for only two or three seconds before deciding whether or not they want to read them, so the opening head is the most important part. A good banner line will entice the reader if it focuses on a need and a solution. Headlines on the envelope will increase the chance that the letter will be opened. Headlines in the letter will grab the reader's attention. Here are some headlines that have been successful:[10]

> **Double your money back if these aren't the best
> brownies you've ever tasted.**
>
> **How I made a fortune with a "fool" idea.**
>
> **Owners save 30%–50% on fuel with the G.E. oil furnace.**
>
> **How to do your Christmas shopping in 5 minutes.**

Here's a listing of the twenty most persuasive words in advertising.[11] Use them in letters.

| | |
|---|---|
| free | today |
| suddenly | miracle |
| now | magic |
| announcing | offer |
| introducing | quick |
| improvement | easy |
| amazing | wanted |
| sensational | challenge |
| remarkable | compare |
| revolutionary | bargain |

Write several headlines and test-market them before sending out your letter. People will usually like all your clever banner lines when they look at them individually, but prefer one over the others when they see several in a group. Surprisingly, out of five or six good headlines, only one or two of them will "work," or motivate people to read your letter. To get accurate research data, select five or six of your best headlines and ask several people which headline they think would be "most effective," not which one they like the best. This allows them to tell you which line they "think will work" without their worrying about possibly hurting your feelings by telling you what they like or dislike about different lines. Use one of the headlines that people consistently pick.

People read your letters as long as what you say benefits them. Letters don't have to be clever, cute, or funny. Two of the most successful books in history, *Webster's Dictionary* and the Sears Catalog, don't have any jokes.

Pictures of happy customers will generate enthusiasm and add realism to your letter because people relate to pictures and tend to see themselves in them. (This tendency is called projection.) Colored pictures generally have more impact than black-and-white ones because people find color to be more visually appealing so tend to look at colored pictures longer.

Finally, personalize each letter. Letters that start out with "valued customer" or "to whom this concerns" get less attention than those naming the recipient, such as "Dear Mr. McMahon." As the saying goes, "Sending letters to someone gets attention from someone, sending letters to no one gets attention from no one."

# Start the Meeting

You promised the customer a five-minute meeting, so be prepared to finish in five minutes. Be ready, however, for a much longer meeting since that's the usual outcome. You have two goals for this initial meeting: 1) to show the prospect you know *your* business and 2) to show the prospect you know *their* business.

# Show Them You Know What You're Talking About

## You Know *Their* Business

There are lots of ways to show prospects that you know their business.

KNOWLEDGE: "I know about fire codes because I researched them for another sale."

EXPERIENCE: "I was a forklift operator, so I know how important unloading speed is."

EMPATHY: "I understand what you're saying. It must be terrible to have a copy machine that's so slow."

## You Know *Your* Business

You let customers know that you know your business by speaking with authority on your products, company and personal achievements. This is no time to be modest. It's important that prospects know how good you are so they will feel confident about trusting you with their business.

# What You Need Is Information

It's time to ask questions. Ask a lot of them. You need to gather enough information to make your next meeting worthwhile. To do that, ask open-ended questions. Open-ended questions can't be answered in one word, and they give the customer the opportunity to talk. Unless you're pinning down a detail, one-word answers usually aren't much help. Answers to open-ended questions, however, can supply a wealth of information and lead to additional sales opportunities. Compare these:

**OPEN-ENDED QUESTION:** How do you do things now?
**ANSWER:** First, the rep fills out an order form and gives it to

the office manager. Then he fills out a configuration sheet for the technicians. After he finishes the credit check, he makes out an invoice that has pricing and serial numbers on it. The problem is that the salespeople repeat the same information on many different forms. Is there a way to simplify the process?

**CLOSED-ENDED QUESTION:** Do you use a typewriter?
**ANSWER:** Yes.

# Data-Gathering and Emotion-Gathering Questions

Most sales questions can be broken down into two types, data-gathering questions and emotion-gathering questions. Roughly speaking, you use data-gathering questions when you're selling necessities and emotion-gathering questions when you're selling luxuries.

## Data-Gathering Questions

Most people buy refrigerators because they don't have one, or their old one doesn't work anymore. They *have* to buy it. People rarely get giddy with excitement in the appliance section at Sears. Refrigerator salespeople, therefore, tend to ask data-gathering questions such as, "How many people live in the house?" "How much cooking do you do?" "Are you concerned with energy saving?" After they get all the data, they show the customers refrigerator models that will fit their needs.

## Emotion-Gathering Questions

Where luxuries are concerned, the purchase is largely an emotional one. We enjoy buying things like vacations, big-screen televisions, and sports cars. People don't buy $70,000 Porsches because they need transportation. They buy them for the pleasure of driving them. So the Porsche salesman asks emotion-gathering questions such as, "Do you like taking the exit ramp at seventy miles an hour?" "Do you want a top-of-the-line stereo?" "How important to you are leather seats?" When the Porsche salesman knows what luxuries and extras the customer desires in a car, he has the customer test-drive a few models.

## Most Products or Services Are a Combination

Most products or services fall somewhere between a purely necessary purchase and a luxury item, so you'll find yourself having to ask both types of questions. A combination of data-gathering and emotion-gathering questions will bring out both the analytical and feeling sides of people. Here is an example:

| Data-Gathering Questions | Emotion-Gathering Questions |
| --- | --- |
| What's your current system? | How do you like it? |
| What are the things you like? | Why? |
| What don't you like? | Why? |

# Ask About Their Current Vendor

This is a good time to ask customers what they like and dislike about their current vendors and their products. The prospect must not be wholly satisfied with the situation or they wouldn't be talking to you. When structuring your sales efforts, give the customers as many of the things they like as possible, while avoiding things they don't like.

| What Customers Like | What Customers *Don't* Like |
| --- | --- |
| Salespeople who are responsive | Salespeople who ignore them |
| Having phone calls returned | Having to call the rep repeatedly |
| Good service when needed | Poor service when needed |
| Products delivered on time | Excessive delays |
| Salespeople who go above and beyond the terms of a contract | Salespeople who do the minimum required in the contract |
| A wide selection of products | A narrow selection of products |
| Clearly defined prices | "Surprise" charges and hidden fees |
| Reps who are knowledgeable about their products | Reps who don't know their products |
| Reps who help find them solutions | Reps who only take orders |
| Reps who make the system work | Reps who complain that their hands are tied by company rules |
| A fair price | Getting ripped off |

Customers want, and often demand, that their salespeople be responsive. Tom Peters in *A Passion for Excellence*[12] talks about former IBM chairman Thomas Watson's coining the phrase "over-responsiveness." To IBM, over-responsiveness means that when a customer needs action, overwhelm him with attention.

If an IBM mainframe breaks, Big Blue will do everything in its power to get it working. IBM's most important step, from a marketing standpoint, is that anytime IBM does anything for a customer, someone calls to let them know what IBM is doing:

> "I wanted to tell you that the senior engineers have just left Armonk and should be landing at O'Hare in three hours." Or, "The truck with your parts has just left."

IBM realizes that being responsive is just the beginning, and that efforts the customer doesn't know about are a wasted marketing opportunity. Customers won't switch vendors because their rep is too responsive. Customers may switch vendors when the rep, who is supporting them, doesn't report his efforts. There are many forums for telling customers what you're doing for them, including phone calls, memos, and formal and informal meetings. Choose the way that suits you and your customers best, according to their Introvert/Extrovert preference, to make sure they know all the work you're putting in on their behalf. This communication should take place regularly. The time it takes will be well worth it. Many customers are unaware of the work being done for them and will appreciate your keeping them informed.

## Listening

Good questioning skills are only half of the communication process, listening is the other half. When your customers answer you, be an "active" listener. Give them supportive feedback. Agreeing, nodding, empathizing, and questioning when you don't understand something —these responses let your customers know that you're really interested in what they're saying. At the beginning of a meeting ask if it's okay to take notes. Customers will usually say yes and will be happy that you want to remember what they say. If, during the conversation, your mind drifts, tell your customer that your mind strayed and that you missed something of what they were saying. It seems at first as though they would be insulted but, actually, they'll be happy that you want to give them your complete attention and will be glad to repeat themselves.[13]

Here's an example of how active listening works, with a real estate broker questioning a potential client:

> **BROKER:** What are the things you like about your current broker?
> **SELLER:** I like being in the Multiple Listing Service book. The house is being shown a fair amount.
> **BROKER:** What do you like about the MLS book?

**SELLER:** Not only my broker, but other brokers show the house, too.

**BROKER:** That's right. We offer that service, too. Is there anything you don't like about your current broker?

**SELLER:** After people see the house and don't buy it, I like to know why. That way I can make changes, if necessary. My broker tells me it's not important and doesn't call me. I don't like that because, even if my broker doesn't feel it's important, I do.

**BROKER:** Usually there's nothing wrong with a house, it's just not right for a particular buyer. Many buyers don't want to say negative things about someone's home, because they feel it might insult them. Still, if you list your house with me, I'll do everything I can to get helpful information from every person who sees the house.

## Qualifying the Customer—When to Hold 'Em, When to Fold 'Em

When doing data gathering, the most important pieces of information you can get are: 1) if the prospect will buy from you, 2) when they'll buy from you, 3) whether they're financially able to buy from you. This data is obtained during the information-gathering stage by a process known as qualifying. Qualifying is discovering which customers are likely to buy.

Weeding out the tire-kickers is easy. Eliminating customers who are pleasant to deal with and may be big potential buyers is difficult. Your job is to find out, as quickly as you can, if that potential is real. An easy, structured way of doing this is by using the DARN-IT test early in the sales cycle.

## The DARN-IT Test

When qualifying, use the DARN-IT test—Desire, Authority, Resources, Need, Interest, and Timing. Only prospects who have all six qualifiers will buy. Let's look at them:

**DESIRE:** Change is difficult. Do they really want what you sell? Are they aware of any negatives?

**AUTHORITY:** Who signs the check or purchase order? Unless you involve that person in the decision, the sale won't happen.

**RESOURCES:** They don't have the funding or the budget. No matter how much prospects like your product, they won't buy it if they can't afford it. Could you help with financing arrangements?

**NEED:** Is there a cheaper or easier solution or is their current system adequate?

**INTEREST:** What is their level of interest? Is it appropriate at this point in the sales cycle? Are they enthusiastic? Do you really think they're going to buy from you?

**TIMING:** Is your customer going to make a decision in a reasonable amount of time relative to your industry schedule? If they say they're going to buy something in a couple of years, they're not serious.

## Questions That Qualify Customers

Asking customers several non-threatening questions will provide answers that will qualify them, according to the DARN-IT test, without being annoying. Here are the kinds of questions that work:

**DESIRE:** Are you aware that this computer needs to be in a temperature-controlled environment? Have you had experience with my product? Do you realize that delivery time is eight weeks? Did you know that the only colors we have are red and black?

Don't be afraid to let customers know the downside of your product or service. They're going to find it out eventually anyway. If you feel there are legitimate concerns about the viability of what you sell, bring them out here. Customers will sell you on the acceptance of your product, if warranted. Here's an example.:

> **SALES REP:** I really feel that you don't need a car with a turbo engine.
> **CUSTOMER:** I frequently do country driving and my car's too slow.
> **SALES REP:** But the non-turbo version is much less.
> **CUSTOMER:** I know. The turbo engine is only $2,000 more, and I'll get use out of it.
> **SALES REP:** Okay. You know what's best for you.

After working for a company for only a few days, salespeople quickly recognize what objections customers have about their new company's products or services. Customers tend to have the same types of problems. Bringing out common objections quickly will save time.

**SALES REP:** Did you know we only sell Japanese products?
**CUSTOMER:** No, I didn't. Our contract says we can only use American products.

If known or common objections aren't voiced or brought up until the end of the sales cycle, or not brought up at all, a lot of time and effort could be wasted. If this customer had specified "American products only" on the purchase order, the sales rep couldn't sell them anything. Since she found this out in advance, she didn't waste any time.

**AUTHORITY:** Do you make the final decision? What is the ordering process?

Selling to people without purchasing authority means having to repeat the sales process for the decision maker. If your contact isn't the person who is going to make the final decision, include the decision maker in the sales process as early in the cycle as possible. Here's what can happen:

Glenn and Kim have been looking for accounting software, but know that their boss, Cindy, is apprehensive about the idea. They'd like a demonstration.

Maybe Glenn and Kim think they can go around Cindy, or talk her into it later. They're absolutely wrong.

Consider what happened to your competitor, Mark. He spent time evaluating Cindy's accounting methods with Kim. After trying unsuccessfully to get a purchase order, Kim finally called Mark and said, "I can't get an order. Cindy said she wants to wait a year before changing the accounting system. I thought when she saw your system she'd like it as much as we did. Sorry."

That sale was doomed from the start because Mark wasted his time selling to people who weren't qualified. You need to sell to decision makers. In the same situation, you'd be smart to wait for Cindy. If Kim wants a demo, say:

> **YOU:** Sure, I'd like to do a demonstration, but we should include your boss, Cindy.
> **KIM:** Our boss doesn't like or trust the accuracy of accounting software.
> **YOU:** I'm sorry, Kim, but I can't take time to show the accounting system unless we involve Cindy from the beginning. Give me a call when Cindy's ready to see the system.

**RESOURCES:** Do you have a budget? Are you aware of the cost of these systems?

Often customers aren't aware how much products or services cost. You can find out if the amount they want to spend is realistic by asking these questions:

> **SALES REP:** Did you know this car costs $25,000?
> **CUSTOMER:** No, I didn't. I only have $12,000.
> **SALES REP:** Let's look at some sporty $12,000 cars.

Think of the time you would have wasted demonstrating a sports car the customer couldn't afford. By qualifying him, you can direct him to something in his price range immediately.

**NEED:** How do you handle things now? What brings you here?

I cringe when salespeople ask, "What is your problem?" Customers do have concerns and needs but resent having salespeople tell them they have problems.

**INTEREST:** How long have you been thinking about this? Do you know what other systems are out there?

**TIMING:** When are you planning to make a decision?

If the timing is reasonable then proceed; if not, give them general information and tell them you'll talk about specifics when they want to buy.

By qualifying customers, using the DARN-IT test, you'll spend time with those customers who are more likely to buy. As the saying goes, "If you want to hunt ducks, go to a swamp."

After each stage in the sales process, go back and requalify the prospect. Now that you know more about them and their needs, do they still pass the DARN-IT test? If they do, move on. If they don't, put them on the back burner and concentrate on someone else.

# Ask for Another Meeting (and an Order)

If the customer is qualified, ask for another meeting so you can make a presentation. Purchasing agents usually have a few small orders that they haven't placed and will be willing to "throw you a bone" to see how you'll do. Near the end of the meeting you might say,

> "I've talked a lot about service and support and what a good job I could do for your company. What I'd like is a chance to

prove myself. Do you have any small orders that you could place so you can see how good we are?"

If you get the order, great! Even if you don't, if the customer is qualified, you'll want to set up another meeting so you can bring new information, or make a presentation. Making the presentation is covered in the next chapter.

# Conclusion

If you don't know who or where the best contacts are, go to your public library and research them in the business publications available to you there.

Once you have a list of prospects, use in-person calls, telemarketing, letters, or seminars for larger groups—depending on which works best for you and for the customer. Use the following table as a guide:

| Sales Rep's Type | Buyer's Type | Best Method of Contact |
| --- | --- | --- |
| Extrovert | Extrovert | In Person |
| Extrovert | Introvert | Telemarketing or Letter. (Phone calls are okay if they're done at the right time.) |
| Introvert | Extrovert | Telemarketing or In Person. (Introverted salespeople should schedule only a few in-person calls a day.) |
| Introvert | Introvert | Telemarketing, Letter or In Person. (Introverted customers tend to be responsive to Introverted salespeople.) |

During the initial meeting, show that you know your business and their business through expressing knowledge, experience and empathy. Ask data-gathering and emotion-gathering questions to learn if the purchase is a necessity, a luxury, or a combination.

When you sell, weed out the people who *won't* buy so you'll have more time for the customers who *will* buy. Use the DARN-IT test—Desire, Authority, Resources, Need, Interest, and Timing—by questioning the prospect as early in the sales process as possible.

Follow these steps to find, cold contact, and meet with customers:

**STEP 1:** Find the prospects.

**STEP 2:** Know what you sell.

**STEP 3:** Which cold-contact method works best for you?

**STEP 4:** Which cold-contact method is best for the customer?

**STEP 5:** Start the meeting.

**STEP 6:** Show the customer you know your business *and* their business.

**STEP 7:** Gather information.

**STEP 8:** Find out what customers like and dislike about their current products and vendors.

**STEP 9:** Qualify the customer.

**STEP 10:** Ask for an order or another meeting, if they're qualified.

# Chapter 3
# MAKING THE PRESENTATION—GETTING YOUR MESSAGE ACROSS

Incorporating Personality Selling into your presentations insures that they will flow well and that every customer attending will fully understand you. Salespeople who don't Personality Sell often know way in advance what they're going to say. It hardly ever changes. Sometimes they even memorize or read their presentations verbatim during the meeting, no matter what type of audience they are addressing.

Good preparation is important, but Personality Selling will add to the success of your presentation by adapting your approach according to the customer's personality type. It is the second behavioral area used by Personality Selling, the Sensing/Intuitive index, discussed below, that is critical when deciding how to present. This is because Sensates and Intuitives like presentations that are decidedly different.

## The Thing People Fear Most

According to the *Book of Lists*,[14] the American population's greatest fear is speaking in front of a group. The fear of public speaking comes before that of dying, snakes, and getting hit by lightning.

Salespeople, generally, do not fall into this category. In fact, many salespeople find making presentations one of the most enjoyable parts of their job. Because salespeople are usually adept at making presentations, this chapter won't focus on how to give a presentation. It will show you how to adapt your presentation so that everyone will benefit from it as much as possible.

The reason you're having a sales presentation is that the prospects are eager to do business with you. Your initial meeting got them interested in what you have to offer them and your presentation will turn enthusiasm into orders. Your objective, ultimately, is to make a sale and the customer's objective is to buy something he needs. This means you both go into the meeting with complementary goals.

# What Customers Want

Customers want to buy as intelligently as they can. To do that they'll want to know two things: what benefits and advantages your products have for them, and why they should buy these products from you. As long as you address these concerns during your presentation, any number of presentation styles (serious, funny, simple, elaborate) will be successful. Your own personality should come out when you present, you don't want to change that. What you do want to do is adapt the character of the presentation so that the audience will fully appreciate and understand what you say.

# People Tend to Present the Way They Would Like to Be Presented To

Presenters tend to give the type of presentation that they, themselves, would most like to attend. Personality Selling presentations take your natural presentation *giving* style and adapt it to the audience's natural presentation *attending* style. If you have ever found someone else's presentation to be uninteresting and boring, chances are it was because he or she was presenting against your own style. Other members of the audience, who shared the presenter's style, probably thought that the very same presentation was fascinating, clear, and useful. Personality Selling could have made that presentation useful and interesting to all personality types in the audience. A knowledge of the Sensing/Intuitive index is an important part of making winning presentations. Let's look at it.

# The Sensing/Intuitive Index

The second behavioral area important to Personality Selling is the Sensing/Intuitive index. It is useful, in making presentations, because Sensates and Intuitives look at things, and want to be presented to, much differently.

To illustrate an important difference between Sensates and Intuitives, put an apple on the table and ask someone to "list all the words that describe your concept of an apple."

Sensates will use their five senses to describe the apple. They'll tell you how it looks, feels, tastes, what it sounds like when you bite into it, etc.

Intuitives will use their imagination and tell you what associations they link with the apple. They'll say computers (Apple computers), William Tell, Adam and Eve, New York, grandmother's house, etc., but may never mention that the apple is red. They know it's red, or round, or sweet, but won't list these because they're not important to them.

The Sensates will describe the apple on the table, while the Intuitives will describe apples in general. Here's a breakdown of what each type looks for:

| Sensing | Intuitive |
| --- | --- |
| Wants the facts | Wants the concept |
| Needs the practicability | Likes innovations |
| Needs the details | Doesn't want details |

Details and facts are very important to Sensates. According to Robert Benfari, Ph.D., of Harvard University's School of Public Health, "If you give a Sensate a balance sheet, he'll add it up. If you give that same balance sheet to an Intuitive, he'll make a business plan."

The most important aspect of the Sensing/Intuitive preference when Personality Selling is that Sensates need the details of a proposal before they can understand how the solution benefits them. They'll consider presentations without facts or details meaningless. Sensates prefer written data rich in facts that they can analyze.

Intuitives, on the other hand, need to have the big picture first. Details up front will be ignored. Intuitives will think that presentations with too many facts and details are tedious and boring. Intuitives prefer charts and graphs prepared with the big picture in mind.

Of course, Introverted Sensates and Intuitives like having information they can look at alone, while Extroverted Sensates and Intuitives prefer to talk about the written data.

Which type are you? Answer the following questions, and find out:

**DIRECTIONS:** Read each of these ten items and circle either answer A or B, depending on which response fits you best. There are no right, wrong, or better answers. You'll find the key to scoring at the end of this series of questions.

1. **Which is the most convincing to you?**
   A) a presentation with a strong overview.
   B) a presentation with a lot of facts.
2. **When learning a new concept, you think a lot of details first:**
   A) are overwhelming.
   B) are essential to understanding.

3. **When describing something, do you usually:**
   A) describe it factually.
   B) describe it conceptually.
4. **If someone made a presentation to you that had spelling mistakes in it, would you:**
   A) probably not notice or be bothered by it.
   B) view that negatively.
5. **Do you tend to:**
   A) notice little things.
   B) not notice little things.
6. **Do you like buying things that are:**
   A) the latest and greatest.
   B) tried and true.
7. **Do you find untried, new ideas:**
   A) interesting and useful.
   B) sometimes interesting, but often unworkable.
8. **When you make a buying decision, would you most want to know:**
   A) how it would benefit you immediately.
   B) how it would fit into future plans.
9. **Would you be swayed more by how:**
   A) concepts relate to facts.
   B) facts relate to concepts.
10. **When faced with a new problem with no predetermined rules and regulations, would you:**
   A) work within the rules established for other company programs, using accepted company procedures.
   B) think of as many solutions to the problem as possible, despite the established rules.

**SCORING:**
Add the **A** answers for questions
3, 5, 8, 10
Add the **B** answers for questions
1, 2, 4, 6, 7, 9

Put the Total here:_____ S/N

If the Total is 5 or more, you're most likely **Sensing**. Otherwise, you're most likely **Intuitive**.

## Occupations Common to Sensates and Intuitives

Here's a list of occupations that have a predominance of Sensates and Intuitives.[15] Again, every field has a mix of personality types. (All accountants aren't Sensing, all actors aren't Intuitive.)

| Sensates Predominate | Intuitives Predominate |
| --- | --- |
| banker | journalist |
| manager | manager |
| accountant | marketer |
| insurance executive | lawyer |
| office manager | cleric |
| teacher (high school) | professor (college) |
| engineer | social worker |
| executive | psychologist |
| military personnel | actor |

The title of manager shows up twice because that position takes in many different fields and has a high predominance of both Sensing and Intuitive types.

When you meet with someone, or give them a sales talk, you will need to know what type they are so that you can adjust your presentation to them. Sensates and Intuitives will expect far different types of presentation, so find out which they want as soon as you can.

# Preparing for the Meeting

Prepare the contents of your presentation based on the customer's Sensing/Intuitive index. If you're an Intuitive presenting to Sensates, remember to include much more detail and practicalities than you would consider important. If you're a Sensate presenting to Intuitives, cut down on the detail, and replace facts and components with theory and the total solution.

As discussed in chapter 2, the means of communication and the size of the group depend on the customer's Introvert/Extrovert preference. Introverts will want short meetings with a few people and Extroverts will want large meetings with plenty of discussion.

# Presenting to One Person

Presentations don't have to be made to a group to be successful. The only people at many fruitful presentations (usually to Introverts) will be you and the customer. Here, write your presentation in advance and when you arrive at the customer's office, let him look at it for a few minutes before you say anything. Let him read it alone while you see someone on another floor, or make up an excuse to wander around the building for a few minutes. After he's had enough time to read through and digest the meat of your presentation, come back, answer questions, and close the sale. Introverts prefer this type of presentation. Personality Selling, in this way, will turn presentations into orders because the Introverted customer will have a chance to fully understand what you have to say.

Extroverts prefer group meetings because they like the interpersonal interaction. While Introverts prefer individual meetings, they are not always practical or possible because many decisions need to be made by a group, collegially. Here's how to present to groups:

**Do pre-sales test marketing of your presentation**

If the customers are Introverts, send them materials a week before the meeting so that they can review them before your arrival.

If the customers are Extroverts, call them and tell them what you are planning to present so you can get verbal feedback.

# The Pre-Sales Meeting or Conversation

Whether the customer is an Introvert or an Extrovert, call or meet with him or her and do some pre-sales work. If you're not sure whether the customer is an Introvert or Extrovert, call and say, "I have a few ideas I'd like you to review before the meeting. Would you like to discuss them or should I send them to you?"

The Introverts will ask to have the ideas sent to them while the Extroverts will want to discuss the ideas with you.

A pre-sales meeting insures that the solution you're presenting is pre-approved when the meeting starts. Here's an example of pre-sales work:

> **SALES REP:** Andy, I just wanted to let you know that I'm planning to propose a complete line of Century oak tables and desks. The total tab is going to be around $500,000 list price. What do you think?
> **CUSTOMER:** I think that's a little high.
> **SALES REP:** What type of discounts have you normally been getting?
> **CUSTOMER:** I don't think I should tell you that before the meeting.

Sometimes customers won't want to tell you important information but, with a little perseverance, you'll get it.

> **SALES REP:** It's important for me to know because, if I can't come close to the price, I will be wasting both our times presenting.
> **CUSTOMER:** All right, we're getting a 25% discount.
> **SALES REP:** Which brands are they using?
> **CUSTOMER:** They're using a brand I haven't heard of that's supposed to be good quality and they're using pine instead of oak.

You've got some raw data, but now let's see how you stand.

> **SALES REP:** How important is price?
> **CUSTOMER:** The price itself isn't important, because we'll pay for quality, but many members of the committee feel that, if they pay retail, they're paying too much and they expect a 25% discount.
> **SALES REP:** I can propose pine furniture, instead of oak, but I feel that it won't have the durability or the look you need.
> **CUSTOMER:** Go ahead with your proposal. If you give a 25% discount, you'll be in the ball park.

Pre-sales conversations have other benefits, too. You've started a personal relationship with the customer that was low-stress because you didn't actually ask them to buy something. As Bill Murphy, one of my sales managers, said, "You need to have a champion in the company working for you. They'll decide whom they'll buy from when you're not around, so you need as many people pushing for you as possible."

You'll now go into the meeting having at least one person who will champion, or support, your ideas. During the meeting your champion will handle the objections of other group members much more vociferously than you can, and will try to close the sale for you. Why? Because of your pre-sales conversation, your champion has taken partial ownership of your ideas. He'll advocate your ideas for you because it's not just your solution, it's coming from both of you.

# Start the Meeting—What Are the Goals?

Before the meeting starts, make sure that you have your presentation materials, that your audio-visual equipment is working, that the audio-visuals themselves can be seen easily from every seat, and, most importantly, that you know what you want to accomplish during the meeting.

**STEP 2: Establish the goals of the meeting**

At the beginning of the meeting review your and your customers' goals and expectations. You might say,

> "First, I'd like to give a brief history of my company and of my experience. Next, I'll review my responses to the action items from last meeting. Finally, I'll respond to questions or concerns about my proposal. Would you like to add anything?"

Write any suggestions made on a white board or a flip chart. This has the double effect of showing the customers that their concerns are important to you and serves as a reminder to you to address these concerns during the meeting.

They might add:

> "I've been mulling over the proposal you sent me, but I'm unclear about your choice of component parts for the project."

> "Good question. I'll add it to the agenda."

An Intuitive audience wants detailed answers after the overview:

> "I'll cover that after the proposal. Is that okay?"

Sensing audiences want questions taken immediately:

> "That's a good question. I'll go over that now."

# What Are the Goals of a Sales Call?

Sales calls can have many different goals. Every sales call won't have all the objectives listed below, but it will have one or several of them:

- Introduce one another
- Gather information
- Answer objections
- Present information
- Demonstrate a product
- Prove a point
- Negotiate
- Handle a crisis

- Explain a position
- Hear complaints
- Tell customers what you're doing for them
- Meet key members of the company
- Have customer meet key members of your company
- Answer questions
- Thank customers for their business

**STEP 3: Find out if the audience wants a Sensing or Intuitive presentation**

No matter what the goals of the meeting are, Sensing presentations start with details and Intuitive presentations start with overviews. If there's a consensus on first giving details or overviews, proceed. If not, give some details *during* an overview. Direct the details to the Sensing members of the group and the overview to Intuitive members.

> "Most would like the details first? Okay. We make our trade show booths out of lightweight corrugated wood with Velcro on the outside. They're expandable for big or small exhibit spaces and the color can be matched to your logo. [This is for the Sensates.] Here are pictures of booths we've made for companies like yours. [This is for the Intuitives.]"

Sensates get the details and practicability that are important to them, and the Intuitives get the quick overview they need. Switching between Sensing and Intuitive presentation styles for mixed groups insures that everyone understands and appreciates your presentations.

**STEP 4: Make the presentation**

As mentioned earlier, salespeople are usually very good at giving presentations. Still, here are a few general tips to make your presentation the best it can be.

1. **Know your subject area well.** You don't have to be an expert, but you do have to have a good working knowledge of your field. You have to establish credibility immediately. Use your knowledge and experience to convince the group that you know your business, and you know theirs, as quickly as you can. The group will listen to you if they think they can benefit from what you say.

   If a salesperson doesn't know his or her products and can't answer basic questions, Sensing members of the audience will quickly assume the salesperson is unqualified. Intuitive audiences will come to the same conclusion, only more slowly.

2. **Maintain eye contact with the audience.** This will keep the audience's attention on you and generally enhance your credibility. (Many people think that if you don't look them in the eye, you're not trustworthy.)
3. **Don't ramble.** Once you've made a statement, don't keep repeating it. This is different from reviewing main points or summing up at the end of the presentation.
4. **Don't fidget.** Many people swear that they don't tap pens or shift from foot to foot until they see themselves on video tape. These idiosyncrasies are distracting to the audience.
5. **Review main points.** Tell the audience what areas you plan to cover and, as each main topic presented is completed, remind them of the main points and any conclusions that may have been reached.
6. **Make sure your audio-visuals are right.** Good audio-visuals will add sparkle to your presentation. Bad ones will be distracting. Good audio-visuals are clear and understandable. Bad audio-visuals are unattractive, messy, unclear, cluttered, or illegible. They detract from your presentation. Audio-visuals come in several types including transparencies, flip charts, white boards, posters, slides, and video tapes. Match the type of audio-visual to the presentation environment.
7. **Prepare a presentation for Sensates differently from a presentation for an Intuitive audience.** Sensates want information that they can look at. It should be pristine, accurate, and show practical and tangible benefits.

   Intuitives prefer non-detailed audio-visuals, like charts. They'll want to know the theory of why your solution works, and they won't be concerned with the components that make it up.

   Whether you're presenting to Sensates or Intuitives, always phrase information in terms of advantages to the customer. Use feature, function, benefit, and advantage.

## Feature—Function—Benefit— Advantage

We know from chapter 2 that hardware stores don't sell drills, they sell holes. That means they sell an advantage (the hole) instead of the feature (the speed of the drill) and function (why a drill that spins fast is useful). People buy because of advantages (a fast drill can drill a hole in hard or soft wood or in metal). Salespeople often point out the feature and the benefit, and assume that the customer will find the advantage, which they sometimes do and sometimes fail to do. Tell the customer specifically *why* what you're selling will be worth the price. Here's how to present, using feature–function–benefit–advantage for a computer printer.

**FEATURE:** What makes your product unique, special, or usable. For example, printers have features like tractor feeds, out-of-paper alarms, long-lasting ribbons, and speed.

**FUNCTION:** What features are good for. The tractor feed's function is to keep the paper aligned while going through the printer so that the type comes out straight on the page.

**BENEFIT:** Uses customers have for functions. Paper is saved instead of wasted because people don't want to send out printed output that's crooked. The printer can also print checks that have small fields on forms that are intolerant of "drift."

**ADVANTAGE:** Why customers part with their money. The advantage is what they'll gain from purchasing your product at this time in the buying cycle. It's the best solution to a problem. Eliminating paper waste will reduce the cost of paper supplies needed. The advantage to being able to print checks is that they'll no longer need the payroll service that has been costing them several hundred dollars a month. They can print out their own checks.

Relating a function, benefit, and advantage to every feature touched on during presentations eliminates customers' thinking, "So what!"

> "This microwave has an automatic turntable [feature]. It insures even cooking [function]. Food won't be well done on the outside and frozen in the middle [benefit]. Wasted meals due to uneven heating will be eliminated [advantage]."

# Audio-Visuals

Here are several types of audio-visuals with examples of when and when not to use them:

**Flip Charts** are effective for meetings of from ten to twenty people, but not for presentations in five-hundred-person auditoriums because they're too small.

**Overhead Transparencies** can be effective when they consist of a few main points (called bullets) expressed briefly. They are also good for showing a picture, figure, or graph. One can easily make a transparency with a copying machine or laser printer.

Warning: Customers tend to quickly lose interest when a presentation consists of a salesperson reading complex and wordy lists from transparencies to them.

**White Boards** are effective when explaining a point. They can be used with multi-colored markers and easily erased for reuse. Their downside is that they can't be prepared in advance, seen in a large meeting room, or used effectively by salespeople with poor handwriting.

**Posters** can be easily transported, are visible to a room full of people, and can be colorful and attractive. The problem is that it is difficult to make changes on them and they can be expensive to produce.

**Video Tapes and Slide Shows** are visually exciting and can be interesting to watch. They can show a product working in environments that customers can't get to or products that are difficult to move. Unfortunately, they are difficult and expensive to change and update with product enhancements. Too, darkening the room could put sleepy members of the audience over the edge.

Experiment with different types of audio-visuals to figure out which are best depending on the auditorium, audience size, product, and the type of presentation you're making.

# Demonstrations

Sometimes you'll need a demonstration to prove that your product does what you say it does. When you demo to Intuitives, sell the "sizzle," or the exciting parts and the big picture. When you present to Sensates, sell the "steak," or the practicalities and facts about a system.

Don't let demonstrations get too bogged down in operations details. Features are very alluring and people may want to spend an excessive amount of time "trying" your product. Intuitives will be happy to see an overview of what it does, but some Sensates will want to see and understand every detail. Even if it is possible to show every nuance of the solution, it is not advisable since you would be spending much more time selling than necessary. The function of a demo is to show how the product works and "sell" it, not to train someone to use it. (Training is saved for after they purchase it.)

> **CUSTOMER:** Before I buy the bookkeeping software, I want you to show me how to set up a chart of accounts for my business.
> **NANCY:** It's important for you to know how to use the software, and when you get it a trainer who knows all of the technical details will spend two days going over how

to set up a chart of your accounts. By the time the training is over, you'll know everything there is to know about how to make the software work with your business. My job is to show you the software's capabilities. It wouldn't be a good idea for you or for me to spend that much time going into the details of running the software program until after you buy it.

CUSTOMER: How can I be sure it will work?

NANCY: That's a good question. We have sample data from a similar business that you can see, and our trainer will be happy to talk with you about what will happen after you buy.

CUSTOMER: Okay.

Have good reasons for setting up more demonstrating time than you think you will need, because what *can* go wrong *will*. Many unforeseen problems can occur during demonstrations, especially when you're adapting your product to the customer's site, or you're working with a prototype. Some customers, especially Sensates, won't see beyond the technical glitches and will make their decision based upon obvious problems with the demo.

# After You've Caught the Bus, Stop Running

When you've convinced the customer your product works, stop demonstrating. Many reps talk their way out of a sale they've already made by overdemonstrating. Let's look at the end of a demo. The salesperson is selling an industrial sorter. The customer is impressed.

CUSTOMER: I'll take it.

SALESPERSON: Let me show you the most powerful part of the sorter. It sorts by customer and town once you've entered the data. Many customers hate doing data entry, but they all live through it . . .

CUSTOMER: Hold on. I think I'll look for a company that does data entry automatically.

Although all the competitions' sorters also need to have the time-consuming data entry done manually by customers, the salesperson's mention of the data entry problem after he got the commitment lost the sale for him. The customer will look for other companies that don't require data entry and may end up buying from someone else.

# Conclusion

Sales presentations give you the opportunity to shine. Structure your call to the audience's personality and cover what's important to customers in the method that best suits the personality type of the audience. Doing this makes handling objections and closing sales, which will be covered in the next chapters, easier and quicker.

For a successful presentation, follow these four steps:

**STEP 1:** Do pre-sales test marketing of your presentation.

**STEP 2:** Establish the goals of the meeting.

**STEP 3:** Find out if the audience wants a Sensing or Intuitive presentation.

**STEP 4:** Make the presentation.

## Selling to Sensates

<u>BEHAVIOR:</u> Sensates trust data they have collected or analyzed themselves. They tend to be conservative and rely on facts. They prefer written proposals to verbal ones. (Extroverted Sensing types will want to talk about the written information, while Introverted Sensing types will want to study it alone.)

<u>WHAT TO WATCH OUT FOR:</u> Sensates lose confidence in the entire proposal if they find typos or inaccurate facts. If the presentation has a messy appearance, Sensates will be distracted by what you say. Many Sensates will assume that carelessness was the reason for factual errors and reason that, if the salesperson was careless with the presentation, he or she would be careless handling their account as well. Some Sensates have eliminated salespeople from consideration for that very reason. If doing a highly detailed, pristine-looking proposal is difficult for you, you're probably an Intuitive. Have a Sensate, who finds detailed proposals natural and easy to do, help you.

New ideas need to be approached with caution since Sensates are more comfortable with established, tried and proven ideas. Sensates want practical, realistic products that are in their budget. They like structure, procedures, and will make responsible buying decisions.

## Selling to Intuitives

<u>BEHAVIOR:</u> Intuitives can become overwhelmed by details. They prefer overviews. When faced with a decision, Intuitives will want to analyze as many solutions as possible.

**WHAT TO WATCH OUT FOR:** Intuitives will consider solutions that don't appear practical, and may explore unworkable possibilities. If their exploration is holding up your sale, show them why the direction they are taking is flawed.

Intuitives love discussing innovative ideas and creative possibilities. Don't be afraid that a solution is "way out." Intuitives like charts and graphs that show the big picture. If you feel your proposals have too many details for your customer, you're probably a Sensate. Show your proposal to an Intuitive first and have him or her help you.

## Presenting to Various Types

**INTROVERTS** want information to study alone. They prefer one-on-one meetings and consider phone calls and unscheduled visits to be interruptions.

**EXTROVERTS** like to talk about solutions and like discussing ideas in groups or committees. They consider unscheduled visits and phone calls welcome diversions.

**SENSING** types want to know details and facts. They'll want to go over each line in your proposal. Extroverted Sensing types will want to discuss every detail of the proposal.

Introverted Sensing types will want to analyze the proposal privately. They prefer written quotes rich in documented data that comes from reliable sources. The proposal should be neatly organized and free of spelling and calculation errors.

**INTUITIVES** will want to know how your products or services will affect the entire company and the future ramifications of the decision they'll be making. Details will be unimportant until the final stages of a decision. Charts and graphs showing the "big picture" will be appreciated.

# Chapter 4
# TRIAL CLOSE AND OBJECTIONS—PERSONALITY SELLING GOES TO WORK

Objections are the barrier to making sales, the reasons people are hesitant to buy. Easing the customer's concerns is known as "handling the objection." In theory and in practice, once you've handled your customer's objections, the customer is ready to buy.

A trial closing and handling objections are part of every sales cycle and can take a very long time or a very short time, depending on the customer. Personality Selling will reduce the time spent handling objections because you'll know the motivation behind the objections and the proper way to respond.

Here's where trial closing and handling objections are in the sales cycle:

1. Gathering information
2. Preparing the presentation
3. Making the presentation
4. Asking and answering questions
5. **Trial Close**          ⟵
6. **Handling Objections**  ⟵
7. Closing
8. Negotiating
9. Delivering
10. Maintaining the account

An important part of trial closing and handling objections is knowing exactly what objections the customers have. The customers' Introvert/Extrovert preference, discussed in chapter 2, which dictated how best to contact them is also the key to questioning them because Introverts and Extroverts think about and respond to questions differently. Let's take another look at Personality Selling to Introverts and Extroverts.

# The Art of Questioning—Introverts vs. Extroverts

Introverts and Extroverts respond to questions very differently because their thought processes are different. Extroverts like to think out loud while Introverts like to think to themselves.

## Questioning Extroverts

Extroverts like large meetings with much discussion and respond to questions immediately, verbalizing their thought processes.

The problem with hearing an Extrovert's thoughts in response to a question means you will often hear contradictory statements or premature ideas. Be careful not to interpret those developing ideas as conclusions. For example, you just asked Cathy, an Extrovert, which of three models of copiers she likes best. She immediately responds with:

> "Well, the model 300 is the best, but the 700 is more expandable. The model 200 seems the right size."

Selling to Extroverts is, in some ways, easier than selling to Introverts, but more difficult in other ways. When Extroverts verbalize their thought processes, what they say is often different from what they mean. In the example above, Cathy spoke about all the copiers. You still don't know, however, which copier she wants, if any. It sounded like the model 200 was the winning copier, since Cathy mentioned it last, but it isn't obvious from what she said: each Extroverted statement often sounds like a "conclusion." After Extroverts verbalize their options, ask one more question: "Which one do you want to buy?"

> "I think I'll get the model 700 because it's more expandable and I need that."

## Questioning Introverts

Introverts prefer to reflect on questions silently. They'll think quietly for several seconds before speaking. For example, you ask Mark, an Introvert, about the copiers. He thinks to himself for a while, debating the question internally, and then says,

> "I'd say we should go with the 700."

Instead of verbalizing each alternative, as Cathy did, Mark thought about it quietly for about fifteen seconds and verbalized only the conclusion. One danger is that interrupting Introverts while they are thinking will halt their thought processes. Introverts need that time to formulate responses to questions. *If you don't allow that time, you won't get answers.*

Too, since you aren't privy to an Introvert's thought processes as you are an Extrovert's, you may need to know how they reached their conclusion. To fully understand an Introverted response, or fill in missing details, ask for clarification:

"How did you come to that conclusion?"

## Two Wrongs Don't Make a Right

Let's look at the right and the wrong way to question Introverts. Greg, an Extrovert, tries selling to Mark:

"Mark, after seeing the model 200, do you have any questions?"

After waiting a few seconds, thinking that his presentation was so clear that no questions are possible, Greg continues:

"I think the 200 is the best one for you. Can I send you a quote?"

Greg has unknowingly cut Mark off in mid-thought, not giving him a chance to formulate any questions.

Mark starts to respond:

"All right, b—"

Greg gives himself the order:

"Great. I'll send it to you tomorrow."

Greg leaves the meeting confident that the sale is his, but in actuality he blew it. Greg missed important objections by not giving Mark time to think quietly. By interrupting him the second time, Greg missed his last opportunity to address Mark's objections. (Salespeople seldom get more than two chances.)

## The Effective Way to Question Introverts

Here's the effective way to sell to Introverts like Mark.

"Are there any questions?"

Wait. Don't assume there aren't any questions. Waiting is difficult for Extroverts, so if you are one, count to ten slowly to yourself.

After thinking to himself, Mark says:

"I'm worried about the cost of paper for this copier. I've heard that inexpensive copiers always use expensive coated paper."

Because you heard the objection, you can address it:

"Modern copiers use plain paper, even the inexpensive ones."

When you trial-close or handle objections, be sure to let Introverted customers speak without interruption. Make sure you know exactly which of the Extrovert's statements are objections and which are developing thoughts.

# Handling Objections and Trial Closing

Now that you've made your presentation and understand how to question prospects, it's time to use that knowledge to handle objections. Handling objections and trial closing are the stages just before the final close. They are grouped together because often the way to know customers' objections is to trial-close them and listen for their response. Here are the steps you use to bring the customer to the closing stage:

## Step 1: Ask for Questions

After your presentation or pitch, ask for questions. Respond in terms of feature–function–benefit–advantage, giving Introverts time to formulate questions. Individually query the group members, especially those who have been quiet. Introverts find large groups intimidating and don't express themselves best in this environment. After everyone's satisfied with your answers, and there are no more questions, go to the trial close.

## Step 2: Begin the Trial Close

The trial close is a soft or easy attempt to get the sale. It's a soft close because its function is really to get the customer's reaction, not the sale. After the presentation, and before you've heard any objections, you ask the customer if they want to buy. You usually won't sell anything at this stage because it's very early in the sales cycle. Customers may still be developing questions or concerns. Occasionally, though, customers will surprise you by saying "yes" when you ask them to buy. Trial closing your prospects is a way to find out, in a non-threatening manner, "where they are."

# When Customers Won't Tell You Their Objections

Sometimes customers will tell you explicitly what their objections are. Then you can answer the objections without delay. When a customer doesn't offer any objections and doesn't give you any buying signals, use the trial close. Trial closing is a way of making customers say if they are ready to buy or not, and why, without pressuring them. If you ask a customer to buy something, they'll either say "yes" or "no." If a customer's not ready to buy, ask why. You can now handle the objections, getting you one step closer to the sale.

There are two types of trial closes: the assumptive close and the trial balloon. The assumptive close comes first and sets up the trial balloon.

The assumptive close is designed to get your customer's reaction. As the name implies, you make a statement that assumes you have the order. If the customer's reaction is positive, both in words and body language, you move on. If it is negative, you go back to information gathering to find out what the problem is.

## Step 3: Begin the Assumptive Close

Here are some examples of assumptive close:

"I'll check how many are in stock."

Negative reaction: "Hold on. I haven't bought anything yet." Positive reaction: "Are there any blue ones?"

"Are you paying in cash or charge?"

Negative reaction: "I don't know if I'm going to buy anything." Positive reaction: "Cash."

## Step 4: Gauge Their Reaction

Sometimes you'll get a non-verbal reaction instead of a verbal response. Watch for it. The appearance of being physically or emotionally taken aback, a sigh, a grunt, or other displeasing sound, and pained looks, all are signs that they're not ready to buy.

## Step 5: Float the Trial Balloon

The assumptive close sets up the trial balloon. The trial balloon is a "soft" close that sometimes gets sales, but its primary purpose is to ferret out objections. The reason you sometimes close the sale at this point is that customers will tell you, "No, I don't have any objections" and "Yes, I'll buy it" before you realize they're ready. No salesperson in the world will be upset that he or she made the sale sooner than anticipated!

For the trial balloon, you want to take control, and not have the customer talk too much. They may be so intent on telling you how lovely your store is, that they never get around to saying, "I'll take it."

Use closed-ended questions, with one-word answers, in the trial balloon and the final close. This is the opposite of the tactic used in the information gathering stage when you want the customer to talk. One-word answers leave you in control because you can more easily direct the conversation if you're doing the talking. Here are some examples:

> "Have I addressed all your concerns?"
> "Are you ready to make a purchase?"

If the answer to either of these questions is yes, proceed to the final close (covered in chapter 5). If you made the sale, write it up. If the answer is no, then go to handling objections, information gathering, or negotiation, depending on the situation.

You go to information gathering if there is still some critical data that needs to be figured into the buying situation.

You handle objections when there's something that is unclear about your solution or there's something they don't like about your product.

You negotiate when customers want to do business with you, but there's no agreement on the terms and conditions, the solution itself, or the price of the solution.

## Step 6: Handle Objections

The reasons customers have for not buying are their objections. Each objection is important to the customer and should be treated as valid by you. Similar personality types tend to have similar objections. Knowing your customers' personalities will allow you to anticipate these objections and handle many of them before the closing stage.

# Put Yourself in Your Customer's Shoes

A good way to anticipate objections is to "walk in your customer's shoes" for a while. What things would be important to you if you were the customer? Be the customer instead of the salesperson for a moment. When you'd be ready to buy from you, you're ready to sell to them. What are the things customers want from their salespeople? Here's what typical customers expect:

1. Good service
2. Knowledgeable reps
3. Dealing with a reputable company
4. Reliable products
5. Responsiveness

Notice what's missing? Price. The issue of price comes far down on the list of concerns. If you're competitive, price is usually a non-issue. Providing these five things customers want will win you as much business as you can handle.

# Wear Your Competitor's Shoes

After you've metaphorically taken your customer's shoes off, put your competitor's shoes on. What if you were working for them, instead of your company? What do they say about their products and about yours? What they offer must be valuable, since they, too, have customers. Lawyers prepare two briefs, theirs and the prosecution's. Salespeople should do the same thing. What are your competitors saying about you? (Many of the same things you say about them!)

They say:

1. Your service is good, but theirs is better.
2. You know a lot, but they know more.
3. Your company's reputable, their company's outstanding.
4. You've got good products, they've got great products and a great selection.
5. You're responsive, but they're obsessive.

When you think like your competitor, then you are ready to handle your customer's objections when they crop up. Experienced salespeople know never to negative-sell, or bash, the competition. There's an old saying, "What goes around, comes around." The reason negative selling doesn't work is that, when people say negative things about the competition, it's the customer's inclination to defend the bashed party and have an adverse attitude toward the source of the criticism (especially so with Feeling types).

Sometimes customers will bait you into negative salesmanship by saying things like, "Why should I buy from you and not from Marta down the street?"

A good response is something like,

> "Marta is a good sales rep and works for a reputable company, but I don't like talking about what the competition can or can't do, but what I can do for you."

# Types of Objections

The types of objections you can expect, and how to answer the objections, are defined by a customer's preference on the Thinking/Feeling index. Let's look at this third behavioral area of Personality Selling. It deals with who or what is important in the buying decision.

# The Thinking/Feeling Index

The Thinking/Feeling index relates to the customer's buying motivations and how they deal with people.

Thinking types view people and things analytically and objectively. Feeling types view people and things personally and emotionally. Thinking types tend to find it easy to think of groups impersonally, while Feeling types view groups as a collection of individuals. Feeling types will buy because people's lives will be enhanced, while Thinking types will buy because it is the logical thing to do.

To find out what type you are, answer the following questions:

**DIRECTIONS:** Read each of these ten items and circle either answer A or B, depending on which answer fits you best. There aren't any right, wrong or better answers. You'll find the key to scoring at the end of this series of questions.

1. **When you make a decision, you are mostly swayed by:**
   A) how you are sure it will turn out.
   B) how you hope it will turn out.

2. **If you are buying something for someone else, are you concerned:**
   A) that you are buying the right thing.
   B) that they will like it.

3. **You like selling to customers who are:**
   A) nice.
   B) fair.

4. **When you buy something, are you more concerned with:**
   A) its cost vs. benefits.
   B) how much people will like it.

5. **When you think about a new target market, do you tend to think of a demographic segment:**
   A) as individuals.
   B) as a group.

6. **If you're at a meeting and two salespeople are arguing, do you:**
   A) feel bad there is disharmony.
   B) assume that interpersonal conflict is unavoidable.

7. **If your company has a price increase that you know will be financially difficult for some customers, would you:**
   A) feel bad they'll be upset about the increase.
   B) assume that price increases are inevitable.

8. **If a customer complained about the company, would you:**
   A) not take it personally.
   B) take it personally.

9. **After trying to make a disgruntled customer happy, with no luck, would you:**
   A) keep trying until you are successful.
   B) give up.

10. **Do you feel your best buying decisions were made:**
    A) rationally and precisely.
    B) emotionally.

**SCORING:**
Add the **A** answers for questions
1, 2, 4, 8, 10
Add the **B** answers for questions
3, 5, 6, 7, 9

Put the Total here:_____ T/F

If the Total is 5 or more you're most likely a **Thinking** type. Otherwise, you're most likely a **Feeling** type.

## Occupations Common to Thinking and Feeling Types

Here's a list of professions and occupations commonly chosen by Thinking and Feeling types.[16]

| Thinking Types Predominate | Feeling Types Predominate |
| --- | --- |
| manager | cleric |
| researcher | preschool teacher |
| programmer | receptionist |
| auditor | nurse |
| banker | office manager |
| credit investigator | librarian |
| steel worker | waiter/waitress |
| scientist | counselor |
| engineer | physician |
| detective | musician |

Thinking-types' objections usually focus on a solution not making sense to them or the cost/benefit analysis not measuring up. You handle Thinking-types' objections by giving them analytical proof that your solution is the best and most logical choice for them.

Feeling-types' objections will be put in terms of the solution not enhancing someone's life, or there will be a difficult transition period. You handle their objections by showing them that your solution will make life easier or better. You do this by either referring the Feeling types to other satisfied customers or by doing a demonstration. Your references will tell the customer that they are happy with the solution provided to them, and a demonstration will let the Feeling-type customer see firsthand how the product will benefit people.

# Typing the Thinking/Feeling Customer

By listening and observing, you'll find out if your customer is a Thinking or Feeling type. Ask, "What are your decision-making criteria?"

If customers say things like, "I want it to be efficient" or "I want to make sure it has a positive risk-return function," they're Thinking types. Unless you can show that happy employees directly affect the end result, don't use that as a selling point.

If customers say, "I won't decide until I'm convinced that my staff will be happy," they're Feeling types. Selling them on cost-savings or efficiency will have limited impact because Feeling types view these types of advantages as much lower priorities than human benefit.

# Handling Objections

Here's how to handle the objections of Thinking types:

> **THINKING-TYPE OBJECTION:** I know that many people think having a fax machine is important, but I can live with the mail service's two to three day delay.

Focus your response on the analytical reasons why a purchase must be made.

> **RESPONSE:** Though you can live with a two to three day delay, many customers can't. If customers need products quickly, they'll often place the order with a company that they can fax. Not having a fax machine will cost you much more business than the machine's purchase price.

When Feeling types have objections, focus your response on the benefits people will derive from the purchase they'll make.

> **FEELING-TYPE OBJECTION:** Sending a fax is so impersonal. People would much rather have me deliver information personally.
>
> **RESPONSE:** That's true. But, there are going to be times when you can't be in two places at once, and your customers may need information quickly. Also, some customers prefer being able to fax information to you. Your having a fax machine would be a convenience to them.

# Handling Objections by Type

Three of the four Personality Selling behavioral areas have been covered so far: Introvert/Extrovert, Sensing/Intuitive, and Thinking/Feeling. Here are common objections you can expect by type.

## Introvert/Extrovert

Extroverts will tell you their objections and discuss solutions, while Introverts will wait for you to ask what their objections are. If you're dealing with a strong Introvert, ask non-threatening assumptive close questions to bring out objections so that you can respond to them.

## Sensing/Intuitive

Sensing types want practical and reliable solutions to objections, supported with details and facts. Take an active role in providing that data. You could say:

"If you're concerned about the tax consequences, why not use my phone and give your accountant a call right now."

There are many ways to solve the problem of getting a Sensate the information wanted. Start the information gathering with the customer before he or she leaves. Do as much of the leg work as the sale dictates yourself. This will prevent procrastination, which often happens when customers are left to tie up loose ends on their own. Calling a knowledgeable expert is often the quickest and easiest way to provide the information. If you're selling to an Introvert who feels that many people will have to be called to get a needed answer, make the calls yourself. After you locate the party with the answer, have the customer call for verification:

"I talked to our accountant about the depreciation schedule for capital equipment and confirmed our figures are correct. If you'd like to call him, his number is 555-1200."

Though Introverted Sensates prefer written information, it isn't always possible to supply them with reliable data in that form. Give some thought to the many ways you have of getting information that they'll appreciate and understand. If in doubt, ask them how they want the data.

Intuitive types will want to know how the solution fits into their plans, but won't want lots of data.

"This chart shows how you'll save money over the next five years."

## Thinking/Feeling

Thinking types like logical solutions.

"See how this works?"

"Let's compare the costs, benefits, and trade-offs of my solution to others you've seen."

Feeling types want harmony when change is necessary.

"Let's have your staff sit in the chairs, and see if they think they'll be comfortable."

# What If You Can't Answer All the Objections?

Since what you sell can't be all things to all people, there will be some objections you can't assuage. Customers know there are trade-offs to be made in any decision, so be honest if the customer wants something you can't deliver.

> "We don't have the chair in your first choice of color, but we do have the style, fabric, and price you're looking for. Would the ivory chair fit in your living room?"

# General Categories of Objections

**1. I can't afford it.** Assuming you've qualified the customer (chapter 2) and he has the money, what he's really saying is, "Your solution isn't worth the money to me." Take a step back. *Is* your solution worth the money? If it is, tell him why. If it isn't, find another solution that is worth the money.

"I'm having a cash flow problem" is a banking euphemism for, "I don't have the money." If they have a real cash flow problem (they can afford the solution, they just don't have the money in one big chunk), then do bona fide financial selling (covered in Appendix D). Breaking the customer's back with monthly payments they can't afford, even when you do the breakdown weekly or daily, is gouging, not financial selling. This type of sales, called slam dunking, discussed in the next chapter, should be avoided.

> **SLAM DUNK SALESMAN:** The cost of the big-screen TV is only five dollars a day, or less than fifty cents per show.
> **CUSTOMER:** Five dollars a day over three years means I'd spend over four thousand dollars for a TV.
>
> **SLAM DUNK SALESMAN:** Don't think of it as four thousand dollars, think of it as 50 cents a show.
> **CUSTOMER:** I'm leaving.

**2. Your competitor is cheaper.** It seems as if there's always someone cheaper. If your product or service is market priced, then find out why the competitor is cheaper.

> **SALESMAN:** Is assembly included in the price of the bicycle?
> **CUSTOMER:** I don't think so.

**SALESMAN:** That's why they're fifty dollars cheaper. That's the cost of assembly, which we include.

If your solution is identical to your competitor's, but theirs is less expensive, say:

> "Our prices aren't the highest or the lowest. We're competitively priced. What you don't get buying from the competition is my support and expertise before, during, and after the sale."

**3. I'm not convinced that your solution is the best one for us.** When customers feel strongly that your solution isn't the best one, there's usually a better solution to be found. Find it together. If you're convinced that your solution is best and they don't think so, they may not understand your proposal fully. Discover what part is not coming through clearly to them.

**4. I'm happy with my current vendor.** (This is what your customers will be saying when competing salespeople call to try to take your account away!) Customers are loyal to the salespeople who service them. Salespeople who call on accounts offering cheaper products or better terms are no match for good support. If you call on customers who are happy with their current vendor, they aren't qualified because they don't pass the interest section of the DARN-IT test (chapter 2). If they don't want to deal with a new salesperson, don't worry. There are a lot of new customers out there and lots of accounts that aren't happy with their current sales rep who are waiting for you to call.

If you still want the account and are willing to wait until the salesperson the account is dealing with quits or finds a new job, ask to be the second or back-up supplier. You'll only get special orders and an occasional "blue bird," but you will be the heir apparent when it comes time to change salespeople.

Another genre of objections pop up when the customer says, "I'd like to think about this for a while." Don't think you've lost the sale, because usually you haven't.

# What If the Prospect Leaves Without Buying?

Customers' leaving before you close them is not a crisis. And it doesn't mean you haven't done your job. Some sales managers would have you hold on to the customer's leg and be dragged across the sales floor to keep the customer from leaving a meeting without a signed contract.

Some people assume that when a customer wants to think about a sale, or isn't instantly ready to buy, there's either something wrong with the customer for wanting to wait or something wrong with the sales rep for not handling the objections. The remedy, these people think, is to "fix" the customer by showing him why he shouldn't wait, or to "fix" the rep by having him put additional pressure on the customer.

"If it ain't broke, don't fix it." There are lots of good reasons why a customer won't buy instantly, but will buy eventually. They are:

**1. Customers want to make sure they're buying the right thing.** People want to make intelligent decisions. It is in the nature of Intuitives, especially, to want to check out all possibilities. If you've done your job by establishing credibility, you will most likely get the order. The Intuitive will want to be certain that buying from you is the best of the choices he or she has. Here's a response to use:

> **SALESPERSON:** Do you have any more specific objections that I could answer?
> **CUSTOMER:** No. You've answered all my questions.
> **SALESPERSON:** Great. Selling is how I make my living and I am happy to spend as much time with you as you need. Would it be fair to ask you to give me a call if you find another solution that looks interesting?
> **CUSTOMER:** I'd be happy to.

The customer has committed to calling you before making a final decision. Most people will buy from you without looking any further but, if people do find another solution, they'll call. For instance, Ellen sells television antennas. Her customer, Nancy, an Intuitive, went home to think about her purchase options and decided that getting cable would be better. Nancy calls her salesperson, Ellen, before making a final decision.

> **NANCY:** Ellen, I decided to get cable instead.
> **ELLEN:** How much is cable?
> **NANCY:** It's $25 a month, but I get sixty-four channels.
> **ELLEN:** You would get an extra twenty channels with cable, but that's only valuable if you watch them. Do you like old movies, sports, or religious programming?
> **NANCY:** No.
> **ELLEN:** Then the antenna would give you the same reception as cable for the stations you watch and, at $75, the antenna will pay for itself in three months. With cable you'll be

getting a bill for $25 sent to your house every month. That's $300 a year.

**NANCY:** You're right, I'll take the antenna.

**2. They're unsure whether other people affected by the decision will like what they bought.** People sometimes buy things emotionally, often as a gift, and after they finish buying they wonder if they bought the right thing. This happens most often with Feeling types. Everyone has seen these people in torment at the cash register wondering if the person it's meant for "will like it."

> **SALESPERSON:** You're buying this pool table for your husband and you're not sure if he's going to like it. Is that right?
> **CUSTOMER:** Yes.
> **SALESPERSON:** You can return the table if he doesn't like it but, let's face it, bringing something back that weighs fifteen hundred pounds is not an easy task. Here's what most people do who are thinking of buying a pool table as a surprise. Bring your husband down to the store tonight, but don't tell him why. When you get here, show him the table. Believe me, you'll surprise him.
> **CUSTOMER:** Okay.
> **SALESPERSON:** I'll take dinner late. Could you be here at seven o'clock?
> **CUSTOMER:** Sure.

First, that customer wasn't going to buy that afternoon no matter how much the salesperson pressured her. A pool table is too expensive and takes up too much room for her to buy it spontaneously.

Second, she'll be back with her husband. She knows the salesperson is waiting to have dinner until after she brings her husband to the store. She's not going to let him starve.

Third, her enthusiasm for the purchase won't wane before 7:00 P.M. Her husband, while at home, may have been ambivalent about getting a pool table, but might get excited and take psychological ownership of the table while shooting a rack in the store.

**3. Some customers delay the sale because they need to get a second opinion.** The easiest way to get people to touch a park bench is to put a "Wet Paint" sign on it. People want to be sure that it's dry. People want to "be sure" when they buy things, too. If Fred is buying a boat and his brother-in-law Steve is an expert yachtsman, Fred would be silly to make an expensive purchase without consulting Steve. Steve won't want to spend days looking at boats with Fred but is willing to inspect the final boat Fred picks. Steve may not give Fred any information the salesperson didn't, but Steve's blessing will make Fred feel comfortable. Fred won't buy without it.

> **SALESPERSON:** Is there any information I could provide you?
>
> **CUSTOMER:** No. I think it would be smart to talk to Steve before making my decision.

The customer is doing what he thinks is the logical thing to do. The salesman knows he's a Thinking type and needs to have Steve look at the boat. Set up an appointment.

> **SALESPERSON:** I'd be happy to show Steve the boat but my schedule is busy. Could you give Steve a call so I can set up an appointment for the three of us to see the boat?

When Steve sees the boat and approves it, the sale will be closed.

**4. Some people delay a sale by saying, "I'd like to look at some literature."** This is a tough one to call. Sensing types need to look at facts in black-and-white before they are confident enough in the data to buy. "Looking at literature" is also a way of giving salespeople the brush-off. These people, in fact, will never look at the literature, but figure that asking for it will appease the rep, which it usually does.

If the customer isn't interested, find out if he or she is qualified (see the DARN-IT test, chapter 2). If a customer's not qualified, then giving out the literature is an amicable way to depart for both you and the customer.

If the customer is qualified, and still wants literature, then find out if he wants the brochure to analyze his decision, or is asking for the information as an excuse to leave. If you think it's an excuse to leave, be honest:

> **SALESPERSON:** Often people take literature and then throw it away. Are you not convinced that the solution is right for you?

If they are Sensing types who are convinced, you've done your job. If they still need convincing, keep asking what their objections are as long as they'll respond with answers.

**5. They want to talk it over with someone else.** Extroverts, especially, convince themselves to buy by talking an idea out with someone. You, as their salesperson, are not an impartial sounding board. After they've talked it out with someone, they'll get back to you.

**SALESPERSON:** Will you call me after you've talked the purchase through with your partner?

**6. They want a chance to think it over by themselves.** Introverts will want to internally debate an issue, often in an environment that makes them feel comfortable. Locking them away in a cubby hole at your location may give them the privacy they need, but often Introverts don't feel comfortable in unfamiliar surroundings.

**SALESPERSON:** Why don't you think about it and I'll give you a call in a few days.

For all types of customer contacts, but especially for the times when Extroverts want to "talk it over" or Introverts want to "think about it," try asking the customer when you should call them. If they say Wednesday, call them Wednesday. If they haven't decided by Wednesday, ask when you can call again. Keep calling until you get a final decision. You won't be considered pushy because they told you to call on those days.

As you can see, there are many reasons why customers don't decide right away. If you can't close the sale immediately, settle for a commitment. The sale will be yours eventually. Commitments include executing any plan of action to get the information customers need to feel comfortable with a decision.

## Step 7: Moving On to the Final Close

After you've finished handling objections and have had a positive response to your trial balloon, you're ready to close the sale. That will be covered in the next chapter.

# Conclusion

Objections are reasons customers have for not buying. When you're in the objection handling stage, follow these steps:

**STEP 1: Ask for questions**

**STEP 2: Begin the trial close**

**STEP 3: Begin the assumptive close**

**STEP 4: Gauge their reaction**

**STEP 5: Float the trial balloon**

**STEP 6: Handle objections**

**STEP 7: Move on to the final close**

You can expect different types of objections from Thinking- and Feeling-type customers. Thinking types base decisions on analytical reasoning, while Feeling types base decisions on personal values and improving harmony. Thinking types aren't smarter than Feeling types, nor are their decisions better, just different.

## Thinking

Decides based on reason
Thinks of groups impersonally

## Feeling

Decides based on personal values
Thinks of groups as individuals

Make sure you've handled all the objections before moving on to the close.

# Chapter 5
# GETTING THE ORDER—PERSONALITY SELLING MAKES MONEY

The hardest thing for many salespeople to do is to take a willing customer, on the verge of buying, and put him over the edge. Salespeople call this closing the sale. Personality Selling has a proven five-step process that brings a logical structure to the close, making closing easy. You can easily adapt the five steps to all customer personality types

After you've successfully trial closed the customer and handled his or her objections, you're well on your way to getting the order. By this point the customer should be just about ready to buy. Your job is to see that they commit to a purchase. Here's how to do it:

## STEP 1: Review the Buying Criteria

First, review the customer's buying criteria. Look at your notes or the flipchart that you used to write down the customer's buying concerns and objectives.

> "You said that you wanted a house with four bedrooms, near the highways, on a quiet street, and costs less than $140,000. Is that right?"
> "Yes."

## STEP 2: Find Out If Your Solution Fits the Criteria

> "Does this house meet those requirements?"

Or ask this:

> "Do you have any questions or concerns about the solution I've proposed?"

Asking customers if they have any questions or concerns is a pleasant way of asking them if they have any more objections. Handle objections until the customers have no more reasons for not buying, or they can live with the specific components of your solution that are not optimal for them.

You've just about made the sale! If you've met your customers' purchase requirements and they don't have any concerns about your proposal, 99.999% of the time, they'll buy.

## STEP 3: Ask for the Order

Use closed-ended questions and use your knowledge of their personality temperament to gauge how strong a close the customer will accept. Here are some closes you can use:

> "Is this the house for you?"
> "Do we have a deal?"
> "Should I write it up?"
> "Will that be cash or charge?"
> "What's the next step?"
> "Can I schedule delivery?"
> "Would you like to buy it?"

Ask one closing question at a time, and wait for the customer's response. Introverts will need at least ten seconds to answer you. Extroverts may need some time, too, especially for important or expensive purchases. Your job, up to this point, has been to identify a need the customer has and provide a solution. You win by making the sale and the customer wins by getting the use of your product or service.

Unless either the customer or the salesperson is a rip-off artist, both will walk away from the deal better off than before the deal.

# The First One to Speak Doesn't Lose

It seems that at every sales training seminar, someone always says, "The reason you should not talk after you ask a closing question is because the first person to speak loses. If you talk, that person will be you. If you wait for the customer to talk, it will be him."

*Nothing could be further from the truth.* The customer should be winning when he accepts your offer, not losing. Yes, the customer should be the first one to speak. But the expression should be, "The first one to speak wins."

After you answer the customer's objections, you need another important piece of information, whether you made the sale or whether you still have more work to do.

## STEP 4: Write Up the Order or Go Back to Objection

Some objections don't become apparent to customers until they take out their checkbooks or realize how much their budget will be depleted. In most real-world sales situations, you'll have to retrace information gathering, objection handling, trial closing and attempted closing a few times before you make the sale. A real-world sales cycle might look like this:

1. Cold-contact the customer
2. Have an initial meeting
3. Gather information
4. Make the presentation
5. Handle objections
6. Trial close
7. Make another presentation
8. Trial close
9. Handle objections
10. Attempt close
11. Handle objections
12. Trial close
13. Close
14. Make the sale

Your job is to keep things on track and moving smoothly. Having to repeat steps is not only normal, it's expected. Don't think that because you had to make a second presentation something is wrong. Since the customer wants you to present again, your first presentation must have been a winner.

# Keep the Sale Moving in the Right Direction

After each step, keep going until you get the sale which, with perseverance, you will get. How much pressure do you use? That depends on the personality type of the customer. The fourth and final Personality Selling behavioral area, the Judging/Perceiving index, answers two questions, "How much should I push them?" and, your sales manager's favorite question, "When are they going to buy?"

# The Judging/Perceiving Index

## When Will They Buy?

Judging and Perceiving types view time very differently. Judging types have a concrete sense of time and like making plans and schedules and keeping to them. When faced with a decision, they seek closure.

Perceiving types have a general concept of time and like minimal schedules; they dislike deadlines or closure.

Judging types tend to keep appointment books while Perceiving types tend to stick reminder notes up around the office.

If a Judging type plans to buy something on Wednesday, he'll buy it on Wednesday, because that was the plan. Perceiving types will wait until they are sure they are making the best purchase. The fact that it's Wednesday would be irrelevant.

When you sell to Judging types, set up a buying schedule with them. They'll usually keep to it. When you sell to Perceiving types, find out what information they need to have, what problems need to be solved, and the sequence of events that need to take place before they'll buy. If they are reluctant to decide on a direction to go with their purchase, reinforce the benefits or necessity of making a decision.

The Judging/Perceiving preference, in combination with the Introvert/Extrovert preference, also determines which of the preferences in the Sensing/Intuitive or Thinking/Feeling indexes is the customer's "dominant function." The type ESTJ (Extrovert, Sensing, Thinking, Judging type) for instance has a dominant, or favorite, function of Thinking, a third-index preference. The ESTP (Extroverted, Sensing, Thinking, Perceiving) type has a dominant, or favorite, function of Sensing, a second-index preference. Dominants, and their related secondary, tertiary and inferior functions, will be covered in detail in chapter 8, "Selling to the Sixteen Personality Types."

To find how you score on the Judging/Perceiving index, answer the following questions:

**DIRECTIONS:** Read each of these ten items and circle either answer A or B, depending on which response fits you best. There are no right, wrong, or better answers. You'll find the key to scoring at the end of this series of questions.

1. **You tend to like days that are:**
   A) leisurely.
   B) action-packed.
2. **When you make an important decision, do you usually:**
   A) set a deadline to decide.
   B) decide when you're comfortable.
3. **When you buy expensive things, they are usually:**
   A) purchased on a whim.
   B) well thought out.

4. **If you made a bad decision, would you feel:**
   A) it was the best decision at the time.
   B) like you were rushed.
5. **If you're given a deadline for making a decision, and there's not enough time, would you:**
   A) allow the deadline to slip until you have all the data.
   B) make it anyway, with the data you've got.
6. **You've just decided on a big purchase. Are you most likely:**
   A) relieved the decision is over.
   B) worried it wasn't the right thing to buy.
7. **If you overload your appointment schedule one day, would you:**
   A) try to reschedule some of the appointments.
   B) try to keep all the appointments, even if it is difficult.
8. **When you're not at work, do you have a:**
   A) concrete sense of time.
   B) general sense of time.
9. **Are you usually:**
   A) late.
   B) on time.
10. **When you have several options, do you**
   A) decide when you are comfortable that you have enough information.
   B) set up a deadline for making a final decision, and then work to get all the information by that deadline.

**SCORING:**
Add the **A** answers for questions
2, 4, 6, 8
Add the **B** answers for questions
1, 3, 5, 7, 9, 10

Put the Total here:_____ J/P

If the Total is 5 or more you're most likely a **Judging** type. Otherwise, you're most likely a **Perceiving** type.

## Occupations Common to Judging and Perceiving Types

Here's a list of professions and occupations commonly chosen by Judging and Perceiving types.[17]

| Judging Types Predominate | Perceiving Types Predominate |
| --- | --- |
| chemical engineer | journalist |
| nurse | surveyor |
| sales manager | editor |
| judge | carpenter |
| dentist | actor |
| steelworker | psychologist |
| banker | athlete |
| physician | restaurant worker |
| teacher | research assistant |
| manager | writers and entertainer |

# Typing Your Customer on the Judging/Perceiving Index

Judging types are likely to object that the solution will take too long, while Perceiving types will object to being rushed into a decision.

You'll know whether your customer is a Judging or Perceiving type by the kind of responses given to questions about time, schedules, and closure. As mentioned above, Judging types will seek closure and try to make definitive schedules and keep to them. Perceiving types will avoid making schedules and setting deadlines and delay closure until they are certain they are making a good decision. Here are some examples with Bob, a Judging type, and Donna, a Perceiving type.

> **SALES REP:** Do you know when you're going to make a final decision?
>
> **BOB'S JUDGING-TYPE ANSWER:** Yes. I want to have a purchase order signed by Friday because we need the new packaging. That means I have to select the vendors and products I'll be using by Thursday, so I have time to get signatures.

Bob's Judging-type answer is characterized by firm deadlines (submitting the purchase order for approval on Thursday and getting it cut Friday), closure (the final decision will be made by Friday), and a firm sense of the timing involved in the steps needed to complete the task by the end of the week (knowing that it takes one day to get signatures).

> **DONNA'S PERCEIVING-TYPE ANSWER:** I'll make a decision on which vendor I'll use when someone can prove to me that the new packaging will not leak during shipping.

Donna's Perceiving-type answer is characterized by an *event deadline* rather than a time deadline. She'll decide after she has proof that the packaging won't burst, which is an important concern. She'll buy when a salesperson presents data that handles her objection. If that proof arrives in a day, she'll buy in a day. If it arrives in two years, she'll buy in two years.

## Quick vs. Careful Decision Making

Judging types, like Bob, tend to make decisions quickly. The company will have packaging materials delivered early next week, although the purchasing process may need to be repeated shortly thereafter because the materials bought were substandard and the packaging burst in shipment.

Perceiving types, like Donna, tend to make important decisions more slowly. The packaging Donna eventually gets will be of high quality, but if the purchasing decision drags on too long, Donna's company could lose money because, without the needed packaging, they were unable to make shipments.

## How to "Close" Perceiving Types

Donna was being truthful when she said that she'd buy after her concerns about the sturdiness of the packaging were taken care of. If the salesperson knows that leaking isn't a problem with his packaging, he shouldn't just say, "Don't worry about that. We've never had that problem before." Instead, he should respond by asking a question.

> **SALESPERSON:** I understand your concern. Although leaking has never been a problem, how could I best prove that to you?
>
> **DONNA:** First, why don't we ship some of our materials using samples of your standard packaging? Second, may I talk with some of your references?

You'll find selling to Perceiving types is much easier if you ask them what their objections are, how important the objection is to them, how you can handle the objection, and, most importantly, what event schedule needs to be satisfied to get the order.

## How to "Close" Judging Types

If Judging types, like Bob, ask you to give them a quotation by Friday, make sure you do it. Keeping to Judging-types' schedules will get their support, while delaying their schedules will annoy them. Judging types tend to make schedules for everything, but won't automatically tell you what their schedules are. To find out, just ask and they'll tell you.

## STEP 5: Handling Lingering Objections

Sometimes customers want to buy, but they are reluctant to decide because of a few remaining concerns they have, called "lingering objections." Lingering objections are usually small details, but they can delay or lose the sale for you. The way you tie up these loose ends is to ask the customer, "If I took care of [whatever the lingering objection is] would you buy right now?" If his answer is yes, then the concession you gave just won you the sale. If the answer is no, then there's more to the lingering objection than meets the eye and you'll need to negotiate (covered in the next chapter) or go back to information gathering (covered in chapter 2).

Usually, it is worth giving a minor concession to seal the deal. If you don't close the sale then, the customer may end up buying from someone else or you'll have to spend time going through a longer than necessary buying cycle.

Here's how to handle the lingering objections of a customer who is happy and almost ready to buy:

> **BROKER:** Do you have any final questions or concerns?
> **CUSTOMER:** I like the house, but there's something about it that bothers me. (This is most likely a Sensing-type objection.)

### INFORMATION GATHERING

> **BROKER:** Is there anything else you wanted in a house that you don't see here?
> **CUSTOMER:** No.

### OBJECTION HANDLING

> **BROKER:** Is the price too high?
> **CUSTOMER:** It's a fair price.

### NEGOTIATION

> **BROKER:** If you could change one thing, what would it be?
> **CUSTOMER:** The color of the kitchen wallpaper. I just don't like it.

Focus on the issue of the kitchen wallpaper. Rewallpapering will add $200 to the cost of a $140,000 house.

**BROKER:** Let's write up an offer with a contingency that the seller has to pay to rewallpaper the kitchen with the paper of your choice.
**CUSTOMER:** Okay.

Go back to STEP 1: Review their buying criteria.

**BROKER:** Is there anything else you wanted that I haven't covered?
**CUSTOMER:** No.

Go back to STEP 2: Find out if the new solution fits their buying criteria.

**BROKER:** Do you have any other questions or concerns?
**CUSTOMER:** No.

Go back to STEP 3: Ask for the order.

**BROKER:** Should we write it up right now?
**CUSTOMER:** Yes.
**BROKER:** Great.

Congratulations! You got it.

Giving this concession was important to the customer, who gets the kitchen rewallpapered, but unimportant to the seller eager to sell her house. If the buyer had walked away, needing time "to think," he may have found another house, losing the sale for both broker and owner. (It is okay to let customers, who have had all their objections handled, have time "to think," as covered in chapter 4, because "thinking things over" is part of the buying cycle for them. But, if you end your sales talk with lingering objections still not addressed and let the customer leave, the lingering objection will fester, and the customer most likely won't buy.)

# What If Lingering Objections Aren't Easy?

Sometimes handling lingering objections takes more than just changing the wallpaper in the kitchen. If handling difficult lingering objections will take a considerable amount of time, make sure you close the discussion on a commitment to buy. Depending on the amount of the sale, you may want to get a performance contract that insures that they'll buy.

**CUSTOMER:** My concern is that the property near the house may be disputed, and I might not hold a clear title. The only way to be sure is to search the land records.

**BROKER:** Is that the only concern you have that's keeping you from buying the house?

**CUSTOMER:** Yes.

**BROKER:** I would be happy to search the land records, but that would take at least three days. How about if we draw up an agreement that says I'll do the research for free. In return, if the title is clear, you'll buy the house.

**CUSTOMER:** That's fair.

If you explain your needs to customers on an adult–adult level, the vast majority will understand you're being reasonable and agree. People know that there's no such thing as a free lunch and are willing to compromise to come to an agreement.

## Only Put Pressure On If You Have a Relationship

The "If I handled that one last objection would you buy?" close works only with customers with whom you have established a relationship. Many salespeople have been taught to ask that type of close even with a new customer early in the sales cycle. Salespeople need to earn the right to ask that type of question.

Some companies force their salespeople to choke out, as soon in the sales cycle as possible, "If I provided (whatever) would you buy right now?" A question like that is perfectly appropriate at the end of the sales cycle, but is completely inappropriate at the beginning. Why? Because early in the sales cycle customers don't know who you are, what you can do for them, the types of products you sell, or the kind of company you work for. There is no way you can get an honest answer to this question until the customer knows you and trusts you.

A man I know named Ed was shopping for a new car and a salesman named Jimmy said, thirty seconds after they met, "The type of car you want isn't on the lot, but if I could get it for you would you buy right now?"

Ed told Jimmy he was a serious shopper and that he'd certainly look at the car. Jimmy said, "I need a thousand dollars deposit, or I can't get it over here for you."

Ed explained to Jimmy, as gently as possible, that only an imbecile would do business with Jimmy or salespeople like Jimmy. Ed told me that Jimmy didn't appreciate the advice because, as he was looking around, Jimmy said the same thing to another man who wasn't nearly as gentle in his response.

## Crunchtime's Hidden Objections

Sometimes crunchtime will bring out new objections. Little things that are bothering the prospect like:

"A red sportscar just isn't me."
"My wife wouldn't appreciate my buying such an expensive stereo."
"I just want to check out a few more things."
"I don't feel comfortable buying the first house I see."

When these last-minute hidden objections surface, many reps try to force or "guilt" someone into buying, which doesn't work. Sometimes customers just need reassurance:

"You belong in a Porche."

Other times they need time:

"If you'd feel more comfortable, look at other houses, but before you make a final decision, could you call me?"

Generally, customers with hidden objections will buy from you, although they won't always buy the item they were initially considering, and not always right away.

## Slam Dunks

Slam dunks are high-pressure closing tactics that, ironically, work on people who don't like high pressure. Slam dunks work like this:

"Would you like delivery Tuesday, or would Wednesday be better?"
"They'll be gone tomorrow, so if you don't buy, you'll be out of luck."

Slam dunks can be more overt. Sometimes a salesman will ask a customer for his name and address and for "identification purposes" needs to see something other than a license, which for most people is a credit card. The salesman's closing statement is:

"I've filled out the order form for you. All we need is your signature."

You would think that most people would tell that rep to go pound sand, and many do. Yet, this salesman is in a power position because most people don't like to make a scene in public.

**CUSTOMER:** Let me think about it?
**SALESMAN:** Okay. I'll be back in a few minutes.

After a short time, the salesman is back and slam-dunks the customer:

**SALESMAN** (sounding extremely nurturing): We only have one left. I can't let you leave without it.
**CUSTOMER:** I guess I'll take it.
**SALESMAN:** Sign right here.

Most states have passed legislation protecting consumers against this type of high-pressure tactic by allowing a three-to-five-day cooling-off period. Customers can return what they bought for any reason during this time. Consumer protection agencies, civil courts, and the Better Business Bureau are flooded with complaints every day from customers who have been slam-dunked.

The technical term for this type of selling is "win–lose." The salesman won and the customer lost. Chapter 7 details why win–lose sales should be avoided. Beyond the ethical reasons why salespeople shouldn't slam-dunk their customers, there are some practical reasons, too:

1. **Laws protect consumers, not salespeople.** Slam-dunkers will lose most court cases. Customers *will* sue.
2. **Slam dunkers won't get repeat sales.** Bad news travels fast. Slam dunkers will be the topic of every one of the ripped-off consumer's conversations for days or weeks to come.
3. **Most people won't cave in to high pressure.** Slam dunking will get a few customers to cave in. The vast majority of people will reject being slam-dunked, but they will respond favorable to Personality Selling, since the sales cycle is custom-made for each individual. Salespeople who Personality Sell have a higher close ratio and happier customers than salespeople who don't.

Remember, slam dunks might get the close. But with the slam dunk come unsatisfied customers angry with themselves for buying something before they were ready, often at terms they regret, and angry with the rep for pressuring them into buying. Angry customers who feel cheated are not the type of customer you want. They'll do everything they can to make their reps' lives miserable including calling them twenty times a day with questions, filing lawsuits, and telling everyone they know or meet on the street what a creep they think the reps are. You may lose sales because the competition slam-dunked someone and you didn't, but think of the legal and support problems they'll have with that customer.

## Use Language Comfortable for You

There are no magic words that will work every time, because every salesperson and every customer is different. Use your natural abilities and the words that sound best to you. Some reps try to be suave, but sincerity works best.

## Make Sure You Don't Sound Threatening

Just because you're asking tough questions doesn't mean you have to sound tough. Television's Ted Koppel is a master at this. When he's interviewing people on "Nightline" he doesn't sound as if he's asking questions that are particularly tough. When you read the transcript of his interviews, however, it's difficult to believe the same person asked the questions. If Ted can ask Presidential candidate Michael Dukakis, "Frankly, Governor, you don't get it, do you?," you can ask, "Have you made up your mind?"

## Avoid Gimmicks

There are a million gimmicks designed and used by slick salespeople who want to con their customers into buying. Salespeople with domineering personalities can wear down customers with passive personalities. In each gimmick, the snake-oil salesperson uses superior verbal skills and charisma to wear down and break the spirit of the unsuspecting customer.

Bullying customers usually isn't that difficult and will yield some short-term sales. However, there will also be long-term problems. Developing collaborative, "win–win" solutions with customers and nurturing a mutually beneficial relationship will bring long-term benefits and as many customers as you can handle. "Catching people in verbal trickery," in chapter 6, details many standard gimmicks and how to deal with them when they happen.

# Conclusion

After the presentation, ask for questions, handle objections, trial close, negotiate, and close. Every sale usually detours back to an earlier stage before concluding with an order.

When closing, follow these five steps:

**STEP 1:** Review the buying criteria.

**STEP 2:** Find out if your solution fits the criteria.

**STEP 3:** Ask for the order.

**STEP 4:** Write up the order or go back to handling objections or negotiation.

**STEP 5:** Handle lingering objections (if necessary).

## Judging and Perceiving Types

Judging types have a concrete sense of time and think it's important to decide quickly. Perceiving types have a more general concept of time and think it's important to decide carefully, taking as much time as they need. Perceiving types have an event schedule that needs to be satisfied before they'll buy.

| Judging | Perceiving |
|---|---|
| Has a concrete sense of time. | Has a general concept of time. |
| Seeks closure in decisions. | Delays closure in decisions. |
| Likes things to be planned. | Likes things to be spontaneous. |
| Has a time schedule. | Has an event schedule. |

## How Judging and Perceiving Types Want to Be Presented To

JUDGING types want the presentation itself to be timely and efficient. The solution needs to fit into their time schedules.

PERCEIVING types will want to make good decisions. They'll allow you as much time as you need to present. Make sure you are as complete as possible, especially when relating to their "dominant function."

# Chapter 6
# NEGOTIATION—GETTING WHAT YOU NEED/GIVING WHAT YOU CAN

Negotiation is the process by which two or more parties come to a mutually beneficial agreement. Each party has something the other party wants and is willing to trade it for what they need. During the negotiation, the negotiators give as much as they can to get as much as they need. All negotiations, from ironing out a contract to labor/management talks, share one goal: having both parties come out ahead of where they were when they started. If that's not the goal of both parties then it is not negotiation that is taking place. Negotiation is called a process because there are several steps to the successful conclusion of a negotiation. During the negotiation process, both parties explain to each other what they can offer the other side, what they need from the other side, and the reasons why both parties will come out ahead when they agree on a deal. This chapter will look at those steps in detail.

## How to Negotiate

There are many types of negotiations including labor/management, political, legal, personal, and business. Personality Selling focuses on a subset of business negotiations that salespeople are often involved in: closing sales, wrapping up contracts, and maintaining accounts. The negotiation techniques and the process of explaining needs, desires, and reasons to negotiate are the same for all types of negotiations. There are three essential ingredients to a successful negotiation: parties willing to negotiate, sincere questioning of each other to discover needs, and a desire to maintain a relationship.

### Ingredient #1: Wanting the Other Side to Succeed

The first ingredient in a successful negotiation is the desire of the parties involved to want or need the other person or group in the negotiation to succeed. If you don't want "the other side" to succeed, then you're battling them, not negotiating with them. Coming to an agreement you know will hurt the other side isn't negotiating:

Jerry West, the purchasing agent from General Controls, knows that eighteen percent is the minimum margin his steel suppliers need to make money. Jerry just signed a contract with United Steel that provides them with a four percent gross margin. Jerry battled United Steel, instead of negotiated with them, because he knows they'll fail to make a profit.

If you ask people what negotiation is, most will respond with the antithesis of negotiation, the definition of debating or battling, saying that it is "Getting as much as you can and giving as little as you have to."

If you want to battle, you tell your lawyer to "sick 'em" or the army to "attack." People go into battle seeking a zero-sum gain, or winner-take-all. The battle plan is to annihilate the opponent and come out unscathed.

Unfortunately, when people battle, both parties generally lose. Most of the time the winner gets less on the battlefield than they would have at the negotiation table. Eastern Airlines vs. the mechanics' union and "wars of attrition" are examples of battles where there were no winners, only losers.

Six months after United Steel started shipping to General Controls, United Steel went out of business. United's competitors had long-term contracts they needed to fill, so they couldn't quickly pick up General Control's business left by United's bankruptcy.

Since General Controls didn't have any raw materials, they couldn't fulfill orders, had to lay off workers, and they, themselves, eventually went out of business. The results of the battle was both parties lost.

Salespeople aren't looking to annihilate their customers, and most customers, unlike General Controls, are simply looking for a fair deal from their vendors. Good negotiation isn't "getting" concessions while "giving" little. Negotiation isn't debating or battling because, rather than having a winner and a loser, good negotiations have two winners.

## Ingredient #2: Sincere Questions

A sincere question is one that you don't know the answer to and want to know the answer to. Prosecutors learn in law school that asking questions they know the answers to is the best way to interrogate and verbally attack people. Sometimes people enter negotiations using the same method.

**SALESPERSON:** Are you responsible for making the final decision?

**CUSTOMER:** Yes.

**SALESPERSON:** May I assume that you want to make the best decision possible?

**CUSTOMER:** Yes.

**SALESPERSON:** After reviewing my solution, would it be fair to say that my solution fits all your needs?

Objection! Badgering the customer! Surprisingly, many customers put up with salespeople bullying them and a few buy from them. If your goal isn't to put your customers in jail, ask sincere questions. They work much better:

**SALESPERSON:** What do I have to do to help you make the best decision possible?

**CUSTOMER:** After hearing your presentation, I'd say you've covered everything that's important to me.

**SALESPERSON:** Is there anything I've left out?

**CUSTOMER:** No.

Sincere questions can be tough as long as the reason you're asking them is to gain useful information. There's no limit to the number of sincere questions you can ask and you can ask them whenever you want. A general rule in negotiations is that sincere questions are always appropriate and insincere questions are never appropriate.

## Ingredient #3: Maintaining a Relationship

Good negotiation is the process of "collaborative problem solving," which requires both parties to want the other to succeed. It also requires that the parties maintain a relationship during the life of the agreement. If a salesperson "out-negotiates" a customer into signing a "win–lose" contract, that customer will try to void the contract. If the customer can't void the contract, he or she won't re-sign the contract at the end of its term. (Chapter 9 focuses on how to avoid win–lose deals and the consequences of salespeople battling their customers.)

With a fair deal, both parties walk away from the negotiation table winners and willing to continue a relationship.

# The Standard of Fairness

A deal is fair when you can honestly say that both parties are coming out equally well and that, given the choice, you would take either side. For instance:

Steve had his house listed for $140,000 and Cindy originally offered him $120,000 for it. They negotiated a price of $135,000.

The deal is fair if: 1) Steve would buy a house similar to his for $135,000 and, 2) Cindy would take $135,000 for it if she were selling the house she bought. If Steve wouldn't buy the house or Cindy wouldn't sell because they thought the deal wasn't fair, then it isn't fair!

# Issues vs. Positions

To make sure that everyone wins, the people negotiating need to explain the reasons that issues are important to them. When salespeople negotiate with customers, the keys to understanding things that are important to the customer is listening to them and information gathering. "Things that are important to them" can be either issues or positions. Let's look at what issues and positions are.

## Positions

Positions are opinions and feelings people have about people, places, things, ideas, or anything else. You can't negotiate positions because all positions are equally valid. You will never convince someone they don't have an opinion about something, because they do. For instance, a woman's opinion is that a manual transmission car is best, while her husband's opinion is that automatic is best. Both feel that their opinions, or positions, are best and both are stating their positions correctly. They could argue until the cows come home about which type of car is better with no resolution, because both are completely right in their statements. She's one hundred percent right that she feels standard is better and he's one hundred percent right he feels automatic is better. You must accept people's positions for what they are.

## Issues

Issues are another matter. Unlike positions, issues can be discussed and adapted. Issues are the reasons people have for what they want. One can usually fulfill these desires in several ways. Although Charlie's position is that he wants to build a fence around his house to keep thieves out, his ultimate need, the issue, isn't the fence but safety from burglars. He can bridge the gap between position and issue only after he discovers that his ultimate desire is the safety of his home.

# Bridging the Gap Between Positions and Issues

## STEP 1: What Do You "Really" Need?

The first thing Charlie should do, once he realizes the issue is safety, is to list things he could do to make him feel safer and stop people from breaking into his house. On his list, he'd write:

*a fence*
*a dog*
*a moat*
*heavy-duty locks*
*an alarm system*

## STEP 2: Go Over the Pluses and Minuses of Each Alternative

• Fences are expensive to install, and will block the view.
• Dogs are a deterrent to trespassers, but are expensive, often noisy, and require a lot of care.
• Moats are expensive, and the neighbors will talk.
• Heavy-duty locks are inexpensive, but can be picked by a professional thief.
• An alarm system is expensive to install, but works twenty-four hours a day and will contact the police if someone tries to break in.

What Charlie is doing is analyzing the alternatives to solutions apart from his wanting to have a fence.

## STEP 3: Select the Best of the Alternatives

Although he originally wanted to have a fence, Charlie needed to analyze the reasons for that choice with the same scrutiny as the other choices he listed. Negotiators call this "separating the person from the problem."

Charlie then reasoned that he liked the view from his house and needed the added safety of having the police alerted if there was a problem. He ended up buying the alarm system.

# Separating the Person from the Problem

Robert Fisher in *Getting to Yes* says to "separate the person from the problem,"[18] This means negotiators should focus on the problem, instead of the negotiators' opinions about the problem. When the parties focus on the issues, it not only makes negotiation easier, it is often the key to making it possible. When people get emotionally involved in an argument, it makes it difficult for them to see beyond their strongly held opinions and negotiation is impossible. Here are some examples of issues and positions:

| Position | Issue |
| --- | --- |
| Your prices are too high. | I need a pine fence, not the more expensive redwood one. |
| If I can't buy today, I'll assume you don't want to do business with me. | I need to hear from your bank to complete the credit application. They haven't called me back yet. |
| Your company hasn't been in business long enough. | I want to deal with people who are experienced, because my project is complex. |
| You're driving too fast. | If something were to happen suddenly, we could be killed. |

As you can see from the position column, each statement can be responded to with a counterposition. "You're driving too fast." will be met with, "No, I'm not." One person absolutely feels the car is going too fast, while the other absolutely feels it is not. They can argue forever and never come to a resolution. Why? Again, because both are one hundred percent right in stating their opinions.

Here's an example. Janet, a Judging type, is the driver and Paul, a Perceiving type, her passenger. They are going up a mountain road. (Judging types tend to become anxious if preset deadlines under their control are not being met, while Perceiving types tend to feel that they'll arrive when they get there.) The speed limit is thirty miles per hour and they are going fifty. They are running late to their appointment, which both want to get to on time.

Janet's goals: 1) to arrive at their destination safely; 2) to enjoy driving around the curves on the road as fast as is safely possible; 3) to get to their destination on time.

Paul's goals: 1) to arrive at their destination safely; 2) to not feel anxiety while being a passenger; 3) to arrive at the destination as soon as is safely possible.

## STEP A: Each asserts a position

> **PAUL:** You're driving too fast. (Paul's position is that going fifty in a thirty-mile-an-hour zone is excessive.)
> **JANET:** No, I'm not. (Janet's position is that it isn't.)

## STEP B: Define terms

> **JANET:** What do you mean by "too fast"? (Information query.)
> **PAUL:** You're going twenty miles over the speed limit. (This is still a position because Paul has simply restated his original assertion as a fact.)
> **JANET:** That's true. (Acceptance of a fact.) But they always post the speed limits much lower than they should be. (This is Janet's position, stated as a fact.)
> **PAUL:** No, they don't. The speed limit is the maximum allowable safe speed for the road. Don't you remember that from your driving test? (Paul is using the Department of Motor Vehicles as a third-party reference to back his opinion.)
> **JANET:** I suppose that's what they say, but they don't really mean it. (Janet accepts the fact that the state thinks she should go thirty miles an hour, but doesn't want to, herself.)
> **PAUL:** The real issue is that I don't feel comfortable going this fast because I feel that I'd have no time to react in case of an emergency. (Two issues are brought out here: 1) reaction time, not the speed of the car, is the first issue, and 2) Paul feels uncomfortable that he, himself, wouldn't be able to avoid an accident in case of an emergency.)
> **JANET:** Would you feel better if you drove us there going thirty miles an hour? (Janet begins collaborative problem solving.)
> **PAUL:** Yes.

# Arrive at the Real Issue

The real issue is: Should the driver travel at a speed that makes passengers feel comfortable, even if the driver thinks it's too slow?

Janet's suggestion would solve their joint primary goal of getting to the destination safely, and she doesn't mind travelling at thirty miles per hour if Paul is doing the driving.

> **JANET:** Okay, then. Why don't you drive us the rest of the way?

Paul and Janet could have argued for hours on reaction time, the car's ability to stop, the effectiveness of equipment, Janet's driving skills, the right of the state to set speed limits, etc. These arguments would have been fruitless, since the real issue was the comfort of a passenger.

When comfort became the issue, the positions of Janet's driving fast and Paul's worrying were replaced by a discussion of what should be done apart from how they felt. They separated the person from the problem.

# Issue-Oriented Negotiation in a Sales Situation

People often say one thing, but mean something different. They insist on a low price, with "no extras," but will worry about repair bills and will need service contracts. For instance, let's say you're a travel agent selling an expensive cruise. You know that the cruise lines are very strict about not refunding money when customers cancel their trips at the last minute. You've had several customers upset when it came cruise day and they weren't feeling well. They felt cheated and upset at you, although you warned them of the dangers of restrictive fares. You don't want unhappy customers, but then again many people can't afford the non-restrictive fares and most people don't get sick. Here's how your negotiation goes with Rob, a customer on a tight budget who wants a cruise.

**STEP A: The customer asserts his position**

> "I want the lowest price on the cruise to South America." (Rob's position is that he wants a low price.)

**STEP B: You bring information**

> "The very lowest prices are prepaid and noncancellable." (You let him know a fact he may not be aware of, showing him the flaws in his position.)

**STEP C: The customer asserts his second position**

> "That's all right, I'm not going to cancel." (Rob gives a reason the low-priced ticket is best for him.)

**STEP D: You bring more information that would affect his decision**

"If you're sick, but not hospitalized, there's no refund. If you're sick, you won't want to board the ship."

**STEP E: Discover the issues**

ROB'S ISSUE: He's not planning to cancel the trip and doesn't want to pay a premium fare, but he does worry about getting sick.

YOUR ISSUE: When customers have to make a decision at the last minute due to illness, they will either cancel and lose their money or go and be miserable. You want to protect customers from being put in "lose–lose" situations so that you can develop long-term business relationships with them.

**STEP F: Develop a solution that will satisfy both parties**

COLLABORATIVE SOLUTION: Ron may be willing to pay a little more for the trip, but not as much as the non-restricted fare. He would like security against sudden illness. You say,

"Trip cancellation insurance costs only twenty-five dollars."

His issue about wanting security on a trip he knows he'll take is satisfied, as well as your issue about his being disappointed with restrictive fares. The security is worth the extra twenty-five dollars to him.

"I'll take the insurance and the lowest fare."

Issue-oriented negotiation sounds easy, but it takes practice. If you find that customers are tossing positions back and forth, take a step back and try to find out what the issues are. Then work together to find solutions. The two most common reasons for the stalemating of negotiations is arguing over facts and positions and not recognizing the issues.

# When Arguing Is Useless

ARGUING ABOUT FACTS: Often people will confidently state their opinions as if they were commonly known and accepted facts. Arguing about facts is a form of positional negotiation.

> **SALESPERSON'S POSITION:** 1000 speed film isn't grainy.
> **CUSTOMER'S COUNTER-POSITION:** Your competitor says it is.

Stalemate—until you compare photographs taken with 1000 and 400 film. Only then can you say, "Would you agree that the picture quality is equal?" You need to come to a resolution.

> "We're arguing about something that can be checked out. Let's look at pictures taken with both speeds of film and compare. Then we'll decide."

ARGUING ABOUT OPINIONS: Trying to convince someone that you're sincere is another form of positional arguing:

> **SALESPERSON:** This camera's the best on the market. I love it.
> **CUSTOMER:** I don't really like it that much.
> **SALESPERSON:** I love it! You should, too.
> **CUSTOMER:** That's great. However, the issue is not how much *you* like it, but how much *I* like it.

# Negotiation Tactics

Sometimes people will pretend to negotiate, but are really battling. Robert Fisher, in *Getting to Yes*, discusses the BATNA, Best Alternative To a Negotiated Agreement.[19] The "best alternative" is what happens if there's no deal, or the party you're negotiating with makes offers below your bottom line, or a point below which it's not worthwhile for you to accept the offer.

If you'd be better off without a deal than with one, then don't agree. As the saying goes, "Sometimes the best deals you make are the ones you walk away from."

The best way not to get taken is to know your bottom line well before the negotiation begins. That way you won't get swept up in the heat of battle and agree to something you'll regret later.

Before any serious negotiation begins, make two lists, showing your bottom line and BATNA and your customer's bottom line and BATNA. Some customers want to bring you down to, or below, your bottom line. Here are some tactics they'll try:

RIDICULOUS OFFERS: Some people have been taught, "The first offer shouldn't be accepted" or "Don't take their first offer." To insure this, people make offers that are ridiculously low, or reject good offers simply because the offer is first.

Just because an offer is first doesn't mean it's bad. Accept or reject an offer on its merits whenever it is made.

**CUSTOMER:** I'll give you a hundred dollars for the Cadillac.

Accompany each response with a reason. Responses with reasons are issues, while responses without reasons are positions.

**SALESPERSON:** You know I won't sell a $25,000 car for one hundred dollars,

or

**SALESPERSON:** How did you arrive at one hundred dollars being the value of this car?

GOING BACK TO MY PARTNER: Another way to bring down your bottom line is by your prospect's "going back to my partner" after a deal is made. After finishing a negotiation and finding out what your bottom line is, the prospect doesn't sign because "I need approval." This allows him to return later to re-negotiate, with the agreed-upon price being the maximum. Negotiators call this tactic "good cop, bad cop." The "good" customer says, "I'd take it right now, but my partner needs you to go another twenty-five percent less." Don't be fooled by "good cop, bad cop"—they're working together.

**CUSTOMER:** I'd sign right now, but I just realized my partner would want an extra 10% discount. I'll call tomorrow.
**SALESPERSON:** I won't lower the price because I wouldn't be making enough money. I won't discuss this contract any more unless all the parties are here.

DECIDE RIGHT NOW: The decide-right-now technique is designed to force you to make a deal before you're satisfied you have all the information you need to comfortably decide. This tactic usually takes you by surprise, when you're not planning to decide immediately.

**SALESPERSON:** These are the terms of the contract. Take it now or the deal's off.
**CUSTOMER:** I can't decide on a contract this important this quickly.

Knowing your BATNA beforehand is a big help because you will have thought out the consequences of not coming to an agreement if you walk away. You'll know at any time if an agreement on the table is worth taking because you will have thought it out when you weren't "under pressure." Any deal can be decided upon tomorrow.

CONFUSING THE ISSUE: Confusing the issue happens when a contract is complex, but is treated as straightforward.

**(UNSCRUPULOUS) SALESPERSON:** Just sign this, every-body does.
**CUSTOMER:** Let me have my attorney look at it.

The key to good negotiation is listening. Salespeople tend to be good listeners. Hone those skills, and use them during negotiations. You'll wind up with deals in which everyone wins.

# Catching People in Verbal Trickery

When certain arguments appear to sound fine, but they leave a lingering feeling that something isn't right, it's the result of verbal trickery, or faulty reasoning.[20] The strategy of verbal trickery is to catch you off guard and pressure you into a premature decision. The person using verbal trickery tries to talk you into deciding while you're still unsure about the arguments. This type of negotiation often works because the flaws of the arguments are well disguised and sound convincing.

Here are some examples of verbal trickery in various situations and responses that will help to keep the sales process on track:

**BREAKING THE CAMEL'S BACK:** Assuming small increments are un-important.

> **CUSTOMER:** Their printing press is only one hundred dol-lars a month more than yours.
> **SALESPERSON** (focusing on the total amount): Paying a hundred dollars a month more for seven years makes their press over $8,000 more expensive.

Some reps break monthly pricing down into weeks, days, or even hours.

> **SALESPERSON:** This refrigerator rents for only five dollars a day.
> **COMPETING SALESPERSON:** Did you know that that's over $1,500 per year for an appliance that costs $600 to buy?

This reasoning also comes up in reverse, putting too much emphasis on small increments.

> **VIDEO STORE CLERK:** Renting movies now is a bargain. Prices are lower by ten percent.
> **CUSTOMER:** The price only dropped ten cents.

**ARGUING IN A CIRCLE:** This happens when people state conclusions as arguments.

**BUSINESS DIRECTORY SALESPERSON:** Look at the ad on page 23 of the phone book. It says that our yellow pages are the best.

**COMPETING SALESPERSON:** You're telling me they are the best because they say they're the best. So what? Anyone can make claims about themselves. The claims must be substantiated by other proof.

LOGICAL LEAP: A logical leap happens when people try to get others to draw conclusions without supporting evidence.

**SALESPERSON:** Our company has excellent typewriters. Obviously our copiers are good, too.

**COMPETING SALESPERSON:** There's no similarity between copier and typewriter technology. Having good typewriters doesn't guarantee you have good copiers.

LOADED STATEMENT: A loaded statement is a conclusion presented as fact. Then the person builds upon that "fact," often with correct reasoning.

**SALESPERSON:** People have done more business with us over the years because of our steadfast commitment to quality, service, and value.

There are two loaded statements here. The first is whether, in fact, people *have* done more business with them, and secondly, whether the reasons are the commitments to quality, etc.

**COMPETING SALESPERSON:** If you look at our annual report, it clearly shows our revenues were greater than theirs for the past five years straight.

PERSONAL ATTACK: This is when you're attacked personally for something unrelated to the issue being discussed.

**SALESPERSON:** He can't know anything about chemistry, he's only thirty-two.

**COMPETING SALESPERSON:** The issue here isn't age, but expertise. I'm fully knowledgeable about your needs and our products.

SYMPATHY GRABBING: This occurs when people try to sway with pity.

**CUSTOMER:** We like your quotation, but Sam's mother is in the hospital and he needs the money.

**SALESPERSON:** I feel badly for Sam, but you should purchase the best solution for the company no matter if the solution is mine or Sam's.

**QUESTIONABLE SOURCES:** Questionable sources include non-experts, experts in one field giving opinions in another area, or things people read "somewhere."

> **SALESPERSON:** Fawn Hall says these condominiums will last a lifetime.
> **COMPETING SALESPERSON:** What are Fawn Hall's qualifications for making such an endorsement? Only an architect can judge structural design.

> **SALESPERSON:** Jack Nicholas says you'll hit this softball a mile.
> **COMPETING SALESPERSON:** Jack may know about golf balls, but softballs are entirely different.

> **SALESPERSON:** I read someplace that their product is very expensive to repair.
> **COMPETING SALESPERSON:** Until we know what the article said and in which magazine, we can't make any conclusions about the statement's validity.

**BUILDING A STRAW MAN:** People build straw men by falsely exaggerating the importance of side issues and then attacking them as if they were the main issue. This tends to take the focus off real issues that are not easily attacked. (A straw man will blow down in the wind.) In the following example, one lawn mower salesperson tried to convince the customer that a small increase in gas efficiency was important. This was done to divert the customer's attention from the real issue, the cost of the mower.

> **CUSTOMER:** Your competitor said your lawn mowers get fifty-five minutes of operation per gallon of gas while theirs get sixty minutes of operation per gallon.
> **COMPETING SALESPERSON:** That's true. In an average summer you would spend about three dollars more in gas with our mower. That doesn't justify the additional two hundred dollars they charge for their mower.

**APPEALING TO POPULAR OPINION:** Assuming that because a company or product is more popular, it's better.

SALESPERSON: We've sold more cars this decade than all our competitors [which is true], so obviously our cars are better.

COMPETING SALESPERSON: We've been in business for only five years and in that time we've sold more cars than they did. However, the real issue is the quality of the cars we sell and they sell now. I believe you'll find ours to be superior.

RED HERRING: Red herrings occur when people divert attention from the real issue to a side issue. (The red herring is different from building a straw man. Someone builds a straw man to attack a side issue but uses a red herring to cause people to misjudge the importance of issues. During fox hunts, red herrings are dragged on the ground to take the dogs' minds off the foxes.)

CUSTOMER: We need to have a computer with an eighty-megabyte hard disk.

SALESPERSON (who doesn't have such a computer): What you really need is a color monitor.

CUSTOMER: If you don't have a computer with an eighty-megabyte hard drive, tell me so I can look elsewhere for one.

DIVIDING THE BABY: When people decide to "divide the baby," they may assume a middle position or compromise is best. A middle position doesn't mean each party is giving equally, or that what's left will be workable.

CUSTOMER: You want $1,000 for the couch, and I want to pay $500. I think a fair price would be $750.

SALESPERSON (knowing that his cost for the couch is $800 and his break-even point is $900): Just because $750 is a middle point, doesn't make it fair. The couch sells for $1,000 because of its materials and craftsmanship. That's what it's worth.

ARGUING BY AN EXTREME CASE: This happens when people take an exception to a rule as an obvious outcome.

SALESPERSON: Don't buy that exercise bike. What you need is this couch, it's much healthier for you. My Aunt Martha had a heart attack on a bike and died.

COMPETING SALESPERSON: Aunt Martha was an exception. The Surgeon General says that exercise reduces the chance of an early death for the vast majority of people.

**NOT LISTENING:** Prospects engage in "not listening" when, after you exhaustively give prospects reasons why thermal insulation is good for windows, you hear:

> **CUSTOMER:** That's not important.
> **SALESPERSON:** Is there any evidence I could give you to prove my point?

If there is no response, then they don't want to listen, and you are just wasting your time.

**NEWER IS BETTER:** This assumes a "new" product is "better."

> **CUSTOMER:** We don't want your washing machine, we want the new and improved model at Sears.
> **SALESPERSON:** Washing machines haven't changed much in forty years. Their machine and ours are about the same, except theirs is $200 more.

**THE SNOWBALL DOWN THE MOUNTAIN:** This occurs when prospects set up a grossly exaggerated worst-case scenario of events that "could happen."

> **SALESPERSON:** Having non-IBM computers on the network will surely cause your million-dollar mainframe to crash.
> **COMPETING SALESPERSON:** The signals sent out by our computers are identical to IBM PC's, so the mainframe won't know there's non-IBM equipment attached.

**DIVERSION:** Diversion occurs when people use words out of context.

> **SALESPERSON:** Americans died for your freedom. Buying foreign products makes a mockery of their sacrifice by weakening America.
> **CUSTOMER:** The freedom Americans died for includes my freedom to buy whatever products I want.

**TRADITION:** This occurs when prospects do (or don't do) things the way they always have.

> **CUSTOMER:** I don't bowl. I never have.
> **SALESPERSON:** You should try it.

**THREATS:** Threats are warnings. Some kind of harm will come to the recipient of the threat when the warnings are defied.

> **CUSTOMER:** My boss said that, if I stop buying from his brother, he'll fire me.

A strongly executed threat has no response.

**COMPETING SALESPERSON:** If his brother goes out of business, give me a call.

## Responding to Verbal Trickery

Remember that these responses to verbal trickery are designed to keep a discussion moving on track and not to make the party you're negotiating with feel stupid or inferior. If people inadvertently use verbal trickery or fallacious reasoning, and it doesn't affect the outcome of the negotiation, allow the faulty reasoning to go unchecked to avoid damaging the negotiation.

# Preferences and Negotiating

## Introverts and Extroverts in Negotiations

The Introvert/Extrovert manner of responding to questions (discussed in detail in chapter 3) will come into play during negotiations. Briefly, Introverts will need to be given time to answer questions and will verbalize only the conclusion, while Extroverts will verbalize their thought processes, thereby leaving the conclusion in doubt. Avoid the hardball tactic of rapidly firing statements at Introverts. Don't move on to the next point until Introverts have had time to think about and respond to each statement or question. This is a typical problem with engaging Introverts "in the heat of battle."

## Sensates and Intuitives in Negotiations

Sensates will not want to look at varied or new solutions to problems and will sometimes not listen unless factual data is presented. When negotiating with a Sensate, stress the importance of considering as many solutions as possible and not rejecting them out of hand simply because they are new.

Intuitives will sometimes propose solutions that are innovative but not workable or practical. To the Intuitive, stress the need for solutions that have a reasonable probability of working.

## Thinking and Feeling Types in Negotiations

Thinking types find separating people from problems easy, because objectivity is part of the Thinking process. Thinking types need to realize that there is an emotional element to many decisions that needs to be taken into account.

Feeling types make good negotiators because they are excellent at anticipating the emotional reaction people will have to a decision. On the other hand, they need to develop the ability to separate people from their emotions, which does not come naturally to Feeling types.

## Judging and Perceiving Types in Negotiations

Judging types will try to set deadlines and reject proposals that do not fit into those deadlines. If the agreed upon deadline can't be met after an agreement has been reached, ask the Judging type the reason for the deadline and see if a workable solution can be arranged outside the schedule.

Perceiving types will tend to avoid setting up schedules and deadlines. When negotiating with a Perceiving type, ask if an agreeable schedule can be set.

# Conclusion

When negotiating, first bring out all the positions. Then discover what the issues behind the positions are, separating the person from the problem. Finally, work together to develop solutions so that both parties win.

Figure out your bottom line well before the negotiation begins, and estimate what the other side's bottom line is, too.

Finally, be on guard for hardball tactics or verbal trickery.

# PART III
# Personality Selling in the Field

# Chapter 7
# PERSONALITY SELLING CASE STUDIES

Now that you have a good idea of how a complete sales cycle works using Personality Selling, let's look at five different case studies. The first case will be an in-depth look at a sales cycle with three salespeople trying to sell the same thing to the same INTJ (Introverted, Intuitive, Thinking, Judging) customer. This case focuses on the Introvert/Extrovert and Sensing/Intuitive preferences. One rep uses Personality Selling, while the other two use other sales methods to try to get the business.

## Case Study I—How Personality Selling Works

Let's see how three sales reps, working for different printing companies, go after and try to get a big forms contract. The customer is Bill Drake, operations manager at Empire Mutual, who is responsible for buying one and a half million pre-printed forms a year.

The salespeople are: Jim from Omega Printing, Joe from AAA Printing, and Ralph from The Print Shop. Each met separately with Bill to qualify him and scheduled a follow-up meeting.

### The Three Reps
The personality profiles of Jim, Joe, and Ralph are as follows:

**JIM FROM OMEGA PRINTING:** Jim is an ESTP (Extroverted, Sensing, Thinking, Perceiving) type and will: 1) talk about the order (Extrovert), 2) go into a detailed proposal, line by line (Sensing), 3) assume if his proposal is the cheapest, he'll get the business (how a Thinking type thinks), and 4) not have specific time schedules in mind when he sells (Perceiving). Jim does **not** Personality Sell.

**JOE FROM AAA PRINTING:** Joe is an ESTJ (Extroverted, Sensing, Thinking, Judging type). Joe, like other ESTJ's, will: 1) want to discuss proposals (Extrovert), 2) go into a detailed proposal, line by line (Sensing), 3) assume since his company has the highest volume of sales, they are the best in the area (Thinking), and 4) want to close on a tight, predetermined schedule (Judging). Joe will **not** be Personality Selling.

**RALPH FROM THE PRINT SHOP:** Ralph is an ESTJ, like Joe is, but Ralph will Personality Sell. He will adapt his sales style to the way his customer wants to buy. 1) Ralph's preference is to *talk* about solutions, but he knows he must let Introverts *see* his proposals before talking about them and allow them time to think after asking them a question. 2) Ralph prefers to talk about the practical side of dealing with The Print Shop and to give customers as many details as possible about the benefits of doing business with him. This is Ralph's Sensing function working, but he knows that, when he deals with Intuitives, he should make sure not to overwhelm them with specifics. 3) Ralph's Thinking function makes it natural for him to provide arguments in a logical, analytical manner. However, he knows that, when dealing with Feeling types, he must focus on the human benefit of the sale. 4) Finally, Ralph's Judging function tends to cause him to create deadlines for closing sales. When he deals with Perceiving types he knows he can't rush them, but instead must help them find the information they need before they will buy, and work out their buying event schedule and keep to it.

## The Customer

Bill is an INTJ (Introverted, Intuitive, Thinking, Judging type). This means that: 1) Bill wants the proposal sent to him so he can review it before the meeting (Introvert), 2) he wants an overview (Intuitive), 3) he wants to know the logical flow of materials (Thinking), and 4) he has a timetable for making a decision (Judging).

## Getting Bill Interested

**JIM'S APPROACH:** Jim, from Omega Printing, is the first to contact Bill. Remember, Jim is an ESTP. He will not be Personality Selling. Jim cold-contacts Bill via telephone while working from his list of insurance companies he got at the library. Bill dislikes getting phone calls, except in the morning. Jim happens to call Bill early in the morning and gets a positive response.

> **JIM:** I'm calling from Omega Printing and I'd like to know if you are interested in dealing with my company for your forms business?
>
> **BILL:** Actually, I do have a contract coming up that you might find interesting. We've decided to centralize our forms

business from the home office. Why don't you come in Wednesday morning?

**JIM:** Great. I'll be there at nine o'clock.

**JOE'S APPROACH:** Joe, from AAA printing, who is *not* Personality Selling, cold-contacts Bill in person. Bill, being an Introvert, dislikes vendor's in-person cold contacts and doesn't give Joe a warm response:

> **JOE** (in person): I don't know if you're aware, but AAA Printing is the number one vendor in the area. We can save you money on your contract. If you tell me the types of forms you use, I can tell you exactly how much you'll save.
>
> **BILL:** I appreciate your coming by, but I'm all set with bids on the forms contract.

Bill, of course, isn't "all set" but wants to get rid of Joe as quickly as he can and brushes him off.

If Joe had asked Bill, "Is this a good time to tell you about what my company can do for you?" instead of making a canned speech, Bill might have scheduled a mutually convenient time to meet. Unfortunately for Joe, although Bill has heard of AAA Printing's impressive record, Bill figures he couldn't stand dealing with Joe because Joe overwhelms him.

**RALPH'S APPROACH:** Ralph, from The Print Shop, is telemarketing and phones Bill at Empire late in the afternoon. Although this is normally a poor time to call Introverts like Bill, Ralph uses Personality Selling to set up the initial meeting:

> **RALPH** (on the phone): This is Ralph from The Print Shop. Is this a convenient time to call?
>
> **BILL:** It really isn't, but does your company handle multi-part forms? We have a large need for them.
>
> **RALPH:** Yes we do, and we have nationwide service, also. Is there a convenient time that I could tell you more?
>
> **BILL:** Wednesday morning is good. But I have a meeting at ten.
>
> **RALPH:** If you have a meeting in the morning, would you prefer to meet later in the day, or right after the ten o'clock meeting?
>
> **BILL:** How about if we meet at one, after lunch?
>
> **RALPH:** Great.

# At the Meeting

Since Joe is out of the running, only Ralph and Jim are left to compete for the order. During their initial meetings, both Ralph and Jim used the DARN-IT test to qualify Bill. They uncover the following data:

**DESIRE:** Bill is in charge of centralizing the forms procurement for Empire nationwide. Bill wants to do business with a local vendor experienced in dealing with corporate accounts. Both The Print Shop and Omega Printing satisfy Bill's requirements.

**AUTHORITY:** Bill will be the person signing the purchase contract.

**RESOURCES:** The total approved budget is two million dollars. Both Jim and Ralph feel that would be more than enough money to cover the expense of their forms.

**NEED:** The company needs these forms to fill out state required insurance claims, and their existing supply will be out in four months.

**INTEREST:** Bill sincerely wants to do business with one vendor, if possible.

**TIMING:** Bill knows he has about thirty days to make a decision.

Jim was satisfied with this qualifying information and returned to his office to prepare a proposal from some specifications Bill gave him during the meeting.

Ralph thought the data given to him by Bill about the forms was sufficient, but wanted some more information about Bill so that he could Personality Sell.

# Personality Selling Questions to Ask Up Front

> **RALPH:** Would you like a detailed proposal or an overview?
> **BILL:** An overview would be better.

Ralph now knows Bill is an Intuitive because Intuitives want overviews. If Bill had said he wanted a detailed proposal, he would have been a Sensate.

> **RALPH:** Would you like to discuss the proposal, or have it sent to you first?
> **BILL:** Why don't you fax it.

Ralph thought Bill was an Introvert because Bill didn't want to have two meetings in a row, but this question confirms his suspicion. Introverts want to look at proposals alone, while Extroverts want to discuss them.

> **RALPH:** Do you have a timetable for making a decision?
> **BILL:** I'll want to have a decision made by the end of next week.

Ralph now knows that Bill is a Judging type and that if he can fulfill Bill's requirements by next week, he'll have the order. This is because Judging types set deadlines for decisions and try to keep to them. A Perceiving type would have said something like, "I'll decide when I'm comfortable that a vendor can handle the contract."

> **RALPH:** How do you think people will feel about having the forms ordered centrally?
> **BILL:** They're mostly concerned with shortages during peak selling periods.

If Bill had said that his concern was that people wouldn't be happy having forms ordered from corporate, or if his concern was that they might not like the forms he picked out, then Bill would be a Feeling type. His concern over shortages is a Thinking-type concern because that concern deals with the logical flow of materials.

## Bill's Personality Type Revealed

In just a few moments Ralph has discovered Bill's personality type. He'll use that information throughout the sale. Bill is an INTJ (Introverted, Intuitive, Thinking, Judging type). Ralph knows to pay particular attention to the way he sells Bill on the two index functions on which he and Bill differ, namely E/I and S/N.

## Jim Makes His Presentation

After the qualification meeting, Jim writes a proposal detailing how Bill could save $52,000 a year in printing costs. Before the follow-up meeting, Jim prints his proposal on high-quality paper, binds it, and has it looking perfect. It is twenty pages long and gives pricing and the delivery times for each of the one hundred and ten different forms Bill needs.

When the meeting starts, Jim goes through his proposal line by line, carefully explaining to Bill each dollar he'd save. Near the end of the meeting Jim asks, "Do you have any questions?" After waiting for a few seconds, which seems like a long time with no response, Jim assumes Bill has no objections or concerns and asks for the order. Bill says he'll think about it and get back to him.

## Ralph Makes His Proposal

Ralph approaches the sale with Bill's personality in mind. The questions he asked to discover Bill's buying style are making all the difference.

First, before the meeting, Ralph faxes Bill the information in his presentation a week in advance. The fax shows the flow of materials from the paper mill to the field offices with the following price information:

> **Total for forms:**     **$200 per 1,000**
> **Discount:**                10%

A few days before the meeting, Ralph phones Bill and asks him if he has any questions or concerns about the proposal. Bill says he doesn't. Ralph knows before going into the meeting that Bill likes his proposal since there aren't any pre-meeting concerns.

At the meeting, Ralph asks Bill if there is anything in particular he wants to discuss. Bill is concerned about distribution.

> **BILL:** I'm not sure that the way you've proposed delivery would be effective during peak selling periods.

Ralph draws a material-flow diagram on a white board and reassures Bill that The Print Shop can keep Bill's company supplied during emergencies.

Ralph asks Bill for questions and waits for a reply. (Bill is an Introvert, so Ralph knows to wait ten seconds or more.) After thinking to himself for about fifteen seconds:

> **BILL:** Omega Printing's proposal is $52,000 cheaper.

## Objection Handling

> **RALPH** (selling himself): I've handled your stationery business for five years and will give your forms business the same kind of attention. The reason that The Print Shop is a little more is that I can't give you the attention you need if we were less. Does that answer your question?
> **BILL:** Yes.

## Assumptive Close

> **RALPH:** When we deliver the forms, they'll always be of high quality.

**BILL:** Good. We're not spending two million dollars on junk.

Ralph got a positive reaction from the assumptive close, so he moves on to the trial close.

## Trial Close

**RALPH:** Are you ready to place an order?

After pondering for a minute, Bill tells Ralph he has the contract.
Jim didn't get the order because he sold to Bill the way he, himself, would want people to sell to him. Ralph, on the other hand, sold to Bill the way that was best for Bill by adapting his Extroverted and Sensing functions to Bill's Introverted and Intuitive buying processes.

## Why Ralph Won the Business

Bill likes overviews and prefers reading proposals before meetings. The spreadsheets and high-quality bound proposals Jim provided weren't important to Bill. Jim likes talking through new ideas, while Bill likes reflecting privately before discussions. Bill's Introverted thought process requires that he have time to reflect on ideas before speaking. Ralph let Bill reflect by faxing the proposal in advance, and he got the order.

## Jim and Joe Aren't Bad Reps

Jim's and Joe's proposals and styles aren't, in themselves, ineffective. Quite to the contrary. Proposals rich in detail and appearance are the only type many customers accept. Some customers hate getting phone calls and love getting visitors. Some people only glance at faxes and want to talk through proposals. Ralph gives those customers detailed proposals and initiates and directs discussion. That's why Ralph, using Personality Selling, regularly wins business the others don't get.

# Case Study II—Perceiving vs. Judging Schedules

This case involves looking at how Judging and Perceiving types spend their day. A lot can be learned about Judging and Perceiving types by the way they schedule their time and make decisions. How is your day similar to, or different from, this daily schedule?
First, let's take a peek at a Judging type's calendar:

| | |
|---|---|
| 7:00 | Bring suit to dry cleaners |
| 7:30 | Get subscription to Wall Street Journal |
| 8:00 | Meet with boss, discuss fourth quarter budgets |
| 8:30 | Meet with ad agency rep, make final decision on logo |
| 9:00 | |
| 9:30 | Meet with rep about new equipment bid, decide on model |
| 10:00 | |
| 10:30 | Final interview with new manager |
| 10:45 | Meet with personnel: re job offer to new manager |
| 11:00 | Staff meeting |
| 11:30 | |
| 12:00 | Lunch |
| 12:30 | |
| 1:00 | Return all morning calls |

And so on throughout the day.

The Perceiving type's schedule is next. Perceiving types tend not to keep appointment books, but will be thinking they have to do certain things.

Sometime during the day:

• Do errands if time allows.
• Be available to the boss so he can drop by and discuss the fourth quarter or anything else.
• Wait for the rep's call on the new equipment bid. If she doesn't call in a few days, check on why.
• Eat when hungry and have free time.
• Return important calls, may have to push some to tomorrow

Attend meetings (possibly written on notes stuck up around the office):

8:30 Ad agency—consider rep's new logo proposal
10:30 Second interview with new manager
11:00 Staff meeting

The Judging type's schedule is precise and includes decision deadlines. For example, the logo is scheduled to be chosen right after the 8:30 meeting with the agency rep. A new manager will be decided on exactly at 10:30. The follow-up interview is deemed "final" before it has happened. The job offer will be announced at 10:45.

The Perceiving "calendar" also lists a meeting with the ad agency. But they'll choose a new logo when they see one they like, not because "It's time."

# Case Study III—Seminar Selling

The third case study is an example of how to set up a successful seminar. Seminars are useful because you have full control of the presentation and can create a positive image for you and your products. Seminars are effective for groups of as few as five or as many as five hundred or more. They can be publicized in person, over the phone, by mail, or in the print media.

It's best to phone either before or after the invitations are sent out. Calling before the invitation is delivered will alert customers that it's coming so they won't throw it out as "junk" when it arrives. Calling after the invitation is received will attract interested parties who may not respond without prompting.

## Gear the Invitation to All Types

Even though you only have one invitation, make sure that everyone who reads the invitation will want to attend the seminar, no matter what their personality type. At first that sounds difficult, but it really isn't. All you need to do is include the following features in each seminar:

INTROVERT/EXTROVERT: Make sure there's group discussion for the Extroverts, and one-on-one time for the Introverts.

SENSING/INTUITIVE: Show practicality for the Sensates and the big picture for the Intuitives. If the audience is not homogeneous, ask them if they want to start with the details or demonstrations.

THINKING/FEELING: Provide cost-benefit type analyses for the Thinking types. Show human improvement for the Feeling types.

JUDGING/PERCEIVING: Provide structure for the seminar itself, and set up buying schedules for Judging types. Provide flexibility in the seminar, and set up general buying schedules for Perceiving types.

Here's an invitation that will draw all types:

> You are invited to an investment seminar given by Saisi Real Estate.
>
> This seminar includes a one-hour presentation on "Finding Investment Properties" with several examples of successful strategies used by our clients, as well as a breakdown of the tax consequences of investing.

Our brokers have had an average of 15 years of experience in commercial real estate. They'll be on hand at the seminar and after the meeting to answer individual questions on investing and how it can make financial sense for you. Several customers will also be on hand to share their experiences.

The seminars are scheduled for February 9, 12, and 19, at 9:00 A.M. and 7:00 P.M. Call today for reservations or register at the door for this free seminar.

Here are the "grabbers" in the invitation for each type targeted:

**EXTROVERT:** A one-hour group meeting.
**INTROVERT:** Private meetings after the lecture to answer questions.

**SENSING:** Detailed breakdowns and fifteen years of experience.
**INTUITIVE:** Examples of how the system works.

**THINKING:** How it makes sense and how it works.
**FEELING:** How investing makes sense for you and having customers on hand.

**JUDGING:** Gives a time commitment (one hour plus private questions), and call today to schedule.
**PERCEIVING:** Several times available, and register at door.

The last important part of seminar selling is target marketing and getting a good mailing list. You can buy lists from any number of companies that supply them, or you can develop your own from information uncovered at the library.

# Case Study IV—The TrackMaker Case

The following case illustrates the Thinking/Feeling process in action. (If you still don't know whether you're a Thinking or Feeling type, you may want to complete the Sales Personality Guide in Appendix A or take the abbreviated version found in chapter 4.) For this reader-participation exercise, you have to make a business decision.

## The Situation

You're the vice president of sales for TrackMaker Corp., a manufacturer of aluminum moldings. Sales were down last quarter. There are several theories to account for that drop: 1) low quotas, 2) the reps, most having families, weren't travelling enough, 3) inadequate product training, 4) a price drop by the competition, 5) a lull in the business cycle.

There's a proposal to increase quotas by fifteen percent. Many managers believe it will take six months for the reps to attain that volume; others believe the reps are selling as much as they can. Currently, seventy-five percent of the reps are under quota, and twenty-five percent of the reps are slightly over quota.

Make the decision. Would you approve the quota increase?

## How Did You Decide?

If you based your decision on profit and thought of the salespeople in impersonal terms, you decided like a Thinking type. If you based your decision on what was best for the reps and found it difficult, even in a fictional case study, to depersonalize the reps and their families, you decided like a Feeling type.

## What Really Happened at TrackMaker?

TrackMaker is an actual company that raised quotas, and made the reps do more travelling. Soon after, reps started quitting. By the time a new sales force was hired, sales were at an all-time low. The competitor's price decrease during an already slow period was the actual reason for the revenue drop.

# Case Study V—Figure Out the Type

This case study is made up of the personality profiles of two prospective customers. Can you figure out what personality type they are from the clues given?

> PERSONALITY PROFILE #1: Lauri Mangin loves her job as office manager for a four-physician office. Her duties include greeting patients, scheduling about two hundred appointments a day, filing complicated medical claim forms quickly, and recommending office equipment for the physicians to buy. She needs to make and keep schedules for herself and the doctors so the office can run smoothly.
>
> Lauri is concerned about maintaining a pleasant working environment and seeing that people are happy with the products she buys for them.

## Lauri's Personality Type

Lauri is an ESFJ (Extroverted, Sensing, Feeling, Judging type). Here are the clues that should have led you to that conclusion:

EXTROVERT: Lauri speaks with two hundred people a day. Extroverts like talking to that many people; while Introverts would find that much human interaction exhausting.

**SENSING:** Lauri fills out hundreds of detailed claim forms a day. Only a Sensing-type person could do, much less enjoy, that type of work.

**FEELING:** Lauri wants the physicians and office staff to like the things she buys and she strives to promote office harmony.

**JUDGING:** The clue that reveals Lauri's Judging preference is that she is constantly making schedules for herself and the doctors.

> PERSONALITY PROFILE #2: Tyler George is a researcher for Biolabs, Inc. Tyler does most of his research alone in the lab. When he buys expensive laboratory equipment, he likes salespeople to send him general information on a few specs that he can review at his leisure.
>
> After he gets the data, he analyzes it to make sure it logically fits into his long-term plans.
>
> Tyler tends to let purchases drag on too long and doesn't like it when salespeople push him to make a decision.

## Tyler's Personality Type

Tyler is an INTP (Introverted, Intuitive, Thinking, Perceiving type).

**INTROVERT:** You know Tyler is an Introvert because he prefers working alone and likes to have information sent to him that he can look over privately.

**INTUITIVE:** Intuitives, like Tyler, like general information, even about technically sophisticated lab equipment. If Tyler were a Sensing type, he would want all the details about the equipment sent to him, instead.

**THINKING:** A Thinking type, like Tyler, will logically analyze the data and make his decision on which equipment to buy based on his analysis.

**PERCEIVING:** You know Tyler is a Perceiving type because he finds making schedules difficult and doesn't like being pushed into buying by salespeople.

There's more detailed and complete information on how to sell to ESFJ's, INTP's, and the other types in the next chapter.

# Conclusion

Find out as much as you can about customers before the meeting so you can adapt your selling style to their buying style. When you have a seminar, write the invitation and structure the seminar so that they will interest all personality types.

# Chapter 8
# SELLING TO THE SIXTEEN PERSONALITY TYPES

Some readers may have already figured out that with four areas of Personality Selling, each with a choice of two preferences or functions, there's a total of $2 \times 2 \times 2 \times 2$ or 16 different personality types.

Each person has one function in each of the four areas or indexes of Personality Selling that is preferred. Those of you who took the Sales Personality Guide, in Appendix A or as incorporated into earlier chapters of this book, or the Myers-Briggs Type Indicator know your own four preferences. Even people who haven't taken these tests can sometimes get a good idea of their preferences just by hearing the descriptions and typing themselves. Interestingly, many people think, for example, that they are Extroverts simply because they like being with people, or they are Sensates because they are practical. People are too complex to judge preferences based solely on one personality cue, because there are Introverts who also like being with people and Intuitives who are practical. Remember, your and your customer's preferences are based on how you usually react to situations. That's why you need to ask your customers several questions before you can judge how best to sell to them.

## Same-Type People Are Different

The MBTI categorizes sixteen different behavior combinations, but there are five billion people in the world and each is a unique individual. People are simply too varied to clump them together into only sixteen groups and expect those in each grouping to act in the exact same way. Personality Selling uses the Jung/MBTI-type categories because they are, at present, the best "predictor" of how people want to be sold to, but this isn't meant to label people or their behavior in every situation.

## What Is Your "Dominant" Function?

Psychologists say that everyone has a "dominant" function and an "inferior" function. Personality Selling is recognizing and adapting your selling style to your customer's most developed or dominant function,

| Preference 1 | Preference 2 | Preference 3 | Preference 4 | Type | Percentage of American Population |
|---|---|---|---|---|---|
| E/I | S/N | T/F | J/P | | |

| Type | Percentage of American Population |
|---|---|
| ESTJ | 14.17 |
| ESTP | 14.17 |
| ESFJ | 14.17 |
| ESFP | 14.17 |
| ENTJ | 4.77 |
| ENTP | 4.77 |
| ENFJ | 4.77 |
| ENFP | 4.77 |
| ISTJ | 4.77 |
| ISTP | 4.77 |
| ISFJ | 4.77 |
| ISFP | 4.77 |
| INTJ | 1.67 |
| INTP | 1.67 |
| INFJ | 1.67 |
| INFP | 1.67 |

*Makeup of personality types*

the one they rely on most, while being careful to avoid selling to their least favorite or inferior function, opposite the dominant on the index. The key to identifying a person's dominant, as well as secondary, tertiary and inferior functions, is his or her preferences on the Introvert/Extrovert and Judging/Perceiving indexes. Extrovert Judging and Introvert Perceiving types have their third index preference dominant; while Introvert Judging and Extrovert Perceiving types have their second index preference dominant.

## Locating Dominant, Secondary, Tertiary and Inferior Functions

The first and fourth index preferences determine a person's dominant, secondary, tertiary and inferior functions (second and third index functions). For IJ and EP types, the dominant function is in the second index and the other functions follow clockwise. For EJ and IP types, the dominant function is in the third index and the other functions follow counterclockwise as shown.

# Always Sell to the Dominant Function

When selling, focus your efforts on the dominant and secondary functions of the customer and away from the inferior function. For instance, an ENTJ (Extroverted, Intuitive, Thinking, Judging type) has a dominant Thinking function and inferior Feeling function. Sell an ENTJ on the impersonal logic of the solution (the dominant Thinking function)

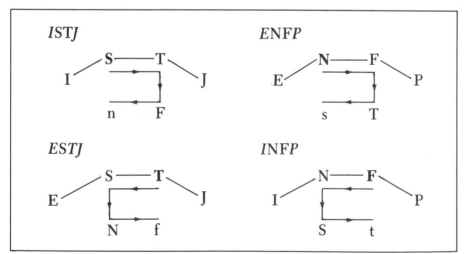

*Locating dominant and other functions*

and not the happiness and harmony the solution will generate (the inferior Feeling function).

It is very important to focus on the dominant function to get the sale. An ISTJ who has a Sensing dominant function won't buy unless all the facts are in hand and he is sure that what he is buying is practical.

# How Perceiving Types Buy

Selling to the customer's dominant function is especially important when you're selling to Perceiving types, because they are careful decision makers. If the product directly relates to the dominant function of a Perceiving type, it's essential to address that function during the sale. If Perceiving types are buying something outside of their dominant function, they'll consider it to be less important and usually make the decision easily.

For instance, suppose a Perceiving type with a Feeling dominant function (INFP or ISFP) is buying office supplies. He will decide quickly, for example, which wastebasket to buy because the wastebasket's color, style, size, etc., won't do anything to affect office harmony or job satisfaction. That decision will be easy. But if that same Perceiving-type customer is buying a puppy for the family, he will agonize over the decision because he knows a puppy can be a joy, bother, or a disaster to a home environment. This customer, with a dominant Feeling function, will be worried about getting the right size dog, with the right temperament, whether to get a male or female, what breed to buy, how hard or easy it will be to care for the dog, what age puppy to get, and if getting a puppy is even a good idea.

When you discover the dominant function of your customers, focus your sales approach to it, and your job will be much easier.

An important point to remember: The function that you *observe*, by the way people behave, is *Extroverted* behavior for both Extroverts and Introverts. You'll notice the dominant function for Extroverts, but the secondary function for Introverts. This concept can be understood with an example.

> ESTP's (Extroverted, Sensing, Thinking, Perceiving types) have a dominant Sensing function and a secondary Thinking function. You can expect them to ask questions about facts but think to themselves, "How logical is this?"

> ESTJ's (Extroverted, Sensing, Thinking, Judging types) have a dominant Thinking function and a secondary Sensing func-

tion. You can expect ESTJ's to ask how logical a solution is but think to themselves, "What details are missing?"

ISTP's (Introverted, Sensing, Thinking, Perceiving types) have a dominant Thinking function that's introverted. Their function pattern looks similar to the ESTP, asking questions about the facts of a system while thinking to themselves, "What's the logical relationship among the facts?"

ISTJ's (Introverted, Sensing, Thinking, Judging types) have a dominant and introverted Sensing function and a secondary Thinking function. This means that their function pattern will be similar to the ESTJ, asking questions about the logic behind the facts and thinking to themselves, "What are the missing details?"

# The Sixteen Different Personality Combinations

## Putting It All Together

Putting all the personality trait combinations together gives more information than examining any single preference separately. Here's how to sell to each of the sixteen different personality types. Each description following covers six different areas of interest to salespeople:

1. **The dominant, secondary, tertiary, and inferior functions.** What you can expect from that type customer and how to adapt your selling technique to the way they want to buy.
2. **The occupations in which the type predominates.** The kind of work and work environment the type likes. This gives you an idea of how best to contact customers in these fields.
3. **Strengths.**
4. **Weaknesses.**
5. **Salebusters.** Actions to avoid. They will annoy or aggravate the customer so much you can lose their business.
6. **How to sell to each type.** This section gives you a template of how a successful sale should proceed. You'll notice that the strategies are far different, depending on the customer's type.

# ESTJ

| | |
|---|---|
| **Dominant** | **Thinking** |
| Secondary | Sensing |
| Tertiary | Intuitive |
| Inferior | Feeling |

**ESTJ OCCUPATIONS:** banker, manager, accountant, insurance executive.

**STRENGTHS:** ESTJ's make sound, practical, and responsible decisions. They'll expect your presentation to make logical sense, but will also be concerned with details.

Neatly organized, practical ideas should be presented to them. New, unconventional strategies won't succeed. They're less concerned about how people feel about a decision, and more concerned with practicality. They won't buy things that are "foolish," impractical or overbudget.

**WEAKNESSES:** ESTJ's tend to reject new proposals and untried products. They might reject proposals based on their appearance, instead of on their merit. They tend not to give positive feedback to salespeople who go "above and beyond," assuming the purchase itself is acknowledgement of a job well done.

**SALEBUSTERS:** ESTJ's are not tolerant of salespeople who can't speak intelligently and confidently about their products. Proposals that are messy, or not well thought out, can lose you the sale. Present traditional, conservative solutions. New ideas need support from factual evidence.

**HOW TO SELL TO THE ESTJ:** Prepare well-organized, neatly presented proposals rich in detail and documentation, and go over them line by line. If you don't know an answer, tell them you'll get back to them, rather than guess. Don't "wing it" because ESTJ's tend to be very good at logical analysis of facts, and one wrong guess can lose their confidence.

# ESTP

| | |
|---|---|
| **Dominant** | **Sensing** |
| Secondary | Thinking |
| Tertiary | Feeling |
| Inferior | Intuitive |

**ESTP OCCUPATIONS:** marketing, police work, construction worker, farmer, auditor.

**STRENGTHS:** ESTP's analyze facts and can understand a large amount of information very quickly. Although they are distracted by "Intuitive" or "unorganized" presentations, they'll look for value in them. They like details but prefer working models over specs.

**WEAKNESSES:** Presentations that rely heavily on theory, have no applications, and don't include models will be a tough sell. If they can't use their dominant Sensing function, ESTP's won't believe that a solution is viable.

**SALEBUSTERS:** Trying to sell new ideas on theory alone. They won't buy unless they can verify that a solution works by seeing, touching, and using it.

**HOW TO SELL TO THE ESTP:** Prepare a thorough, well-organized presentation with prototypes showing practical benefit.

# ESFJ

| Dominant | Feeling |
|----------|---------|
| Secondary | Sensing |
| Tertiary | Intuitive |
| Inferior | Thinking |

**ESFJ OCCUPATIONS:** secretary, teacher, salesperson, nurse, hairdresser, office manager.

**STRENGTHS:** ESFJ's work well with others and are great team players. They're friendly, organized, and realistic. They like harmony and practicality, so usually lead by example. People tend to cooperate with ESFJ's because they want to, not because they have to.

**WEAKNESSES:** The desire for harmony could cause them to avoid areas of conflict. Because they combine factual analysis with human interaction rather than with logical analysis, their decision-making process differs from what is expected in business.

**SALEBUSTERS:** Placing too much emphasis on logic, or "new ideas." Proposing solutions that will inconvenience people, or presenting solutions that will bring short- or long-term stress during transition.

**HOW TO SELL TO THE ESFJ:** Show the benefits people will enjoy and the practicality of buying what you sell. Dress impeccably and fashionably, and prepare a pristine-looking presentation.

## ESFP

| Dominant | Sensing |
|----------|---------|
| Secondary | Feeling |
| Tertiary | Thinking |
| Inferior | Intuitive |

**ESFP OCCUPATIONS:** child care worker, receptionist, transportation worker, engineer, site supervisor, lifeguard.

**STRENGTHS:** ESFP's love being with other people and are adept at noticing details about people and things. They're warm, witty, and outstanding conversationalists. Their combination of realism and concern for others makes them excellent crisis solvers. They'll want presentations and salespeople to be attractive-looking. They'll notice but will overlook missing details.

**WEAKNESSES:** ESFP's like to work in groups and find working alone very difficult. They prefer projects that are practical and have immediate human benefit, and they won't put much credence in analytical and impersonal data.

**SALEBUSTERS:** Sloppy or unattractive presentations will bother the ESFP. Focusing on logic or theory alone will seem cold and won't go over well with ESFP's.

**HOW TO SELL TO THE ESFP:** Prepare a high-appearance proposal and dress classically and impeccably. Focus on facts and human benefits. In-person calls are a "must."

## ENFP

| Dominant | Intuitive |
|----------|-----------|
| Secondary | Feeling |
| Tertiary | Thinking |
| Inferior | Sensing |

**ENFP OCCUPATIONS:** journalist, cleric, social worker, teacher.

**STRENGTHS:** ENFP's tend to be involved in a wide range of activities. They will want to look at as many alternatives as they can and will want to discuss them with you. ENFP's tend not to get caught up in materialism and will buy what makes them happy.

Their inferior function is Sensing and they'll be bored by details and practicality. When making important decisions, an ENFP will look at all the possibilities before deciding. ENFP's are easy to deal with because they tend to look for the good things in salespeople. They are very good at team building and tend to have many and varied interests.

**WEAKNESSES:** ENFP's tend to overlook details about a solution. They may find out later that they made their purchases without carefully examining practicality and find themselves with an unworkable product.

They tend to put off making decisions and change their interests frequently.

**SALEBUSTERS:** Don't overwhelm the ENFP with details. Since they tend to be very sociable, you'll have much more success meeting with ENFP's than sending them something to look at privately. ENFP's will not like it if you ignore how people involved will feel about the purchase or if you refuse to look at alternatives.

**HOW TO SELL TO THE ENFP:** ENFP's will want to talk about an overview of your solution. Because they'll be concerned, assure them that the people affected by their purchase will like it. If the buying cycle gets to be too long, you'll have to let the ENFP know that alternatives can't be examined forever. Show them the benefits of buying sooner rather than later.

# ENFJ

| | |
|---|---|
| **Dominant** | **Feeling** |
| Secondary | Intuitive |
| Tertiary | Sensing |
| Inferior | Thinking |

**ENFJ OCCUPATIONS:** cleric, teacher, actor, writer, counselor.

**STRENGTHS:** ENFJ's make great leaders and see possibilities in people. They encourage harmony and cooperation and are appreciative and adaptable. They're excellent communicators and lead by example.

**WEAKNESSES:** ENFJ's may see too much in people and expect things beyond a person's reach. They may avoid situations that involve conflict. ENFJ's need to make sure plans are logical and practical before undertaking them.

**SALEBUSTERS:** When selling to an ENFJ, don't put too much emphasis on the logic behind a solution, why it should work, or the long-term benefits. ENFJ's will want to see immediate, tangible results and happy consumers.

**HOW TO SELL TO THE ENFJ:** Focus on how products benefit people. Prepare and discuss overviews and have a plan for implementation.

# ENTP

| | |
|---|---|
| Dominant | Intuitive |
| Secondary | Thinking |
| Tertiary | Feeling |
| Inferior | Sensing |

**ENTP OCCUPATIONS:** photographer, marketing, salesperson, journalist, actor, engineer.

**STRENGTHS:** ENTP's are excellent problem solvers and like having challenging, complex problems to work on. They are good at developing solutions to theoretical problems. They lead by example and encouragement.

**WEAKNESSES:** ENTP's are problem solvers but not as good with mundane, non-theoretical tasks. They sometimes underestimate the time it takes to complete a project.

**SALEBUSTERS:** Focusing on details or Feelings or not discussing the proposal.

**HOW TO SELL TO THE ENTP:** Discuss with them theoretical possibilities for the sale. Focus on the big picture and on logic and objectivity.

# ENTJ

| | |
|---|---|
| Dominant | Thinking |
| Secondary | Intuitive |
| Tertiary | Sensing |
| Inferior | Feeling |

**ENTJ OCCUPATIONS:** manager, lawyer, marketing, sales, other problem-solving professionals.

**STRENGTHS:** ENTJ's are very good at problem solving, building structures in organizations, and leading. They like to have ideas presented in logical form, and they are eager to look at many different ways of solving problems. After you sell an ENTJ on an idea, he or she will be very good about following through with a purchase.

ENTJ's are very good at making decisions impersonally, and they need to be aware of the effect their decisions will have on the people involved.

**WEAKNESSES:** ENTJ's are not strong at grasping details and tend to dislike routine. The Feeling inferior function will easily allow the ENTJ to make decisions impersonally. This will make decisions efficient but sometimes unpopular, which could hurt the ENTJ in the long run.

**SALEBUSTERS:** Sending information to ENTJ's with no discussion will get limited attention. Details and facts unrelated to logical conclusions will be ignored and will distract the ENTJ from your presentation.

**HOW TO SELL TO THE ENTJ:** Present several different solutions, and choose the best one in consultation with the ENTJ. The presentation should make logical sense and be forward-looking. Present facts and details only if they are needed for a logical decision. ENTJ's like to talk "solutions" and respond well to buying schedules.

# ISTJ

| Dominant | Sensing |
|----------|---------|
| Secondary | Thinking |
| Tertiary | Feeling |
| Inferior | Intuitive |

**ISTJ OCCUPATIONS:** president, board chairperson, banker, insurance executive, accountant, bookkeeper, adjuster, engineer.

**STRENGTHS:** According to an article in *Fortune* magazine, 35% of all upper-level managers are ISTJ's.[21] ISTJ's have a profound sense of detail and logical analysis.

Their Introverted Sensing makes them adept at analysis. The ISTJ, like the ESTJ, will want conservative, well-thought-out ideas presented clearly and neatly.

ISTJ's will be averse to new ideas because of their traditional mind-set and their Intuitive inferior function. They will tend to view anything not traditional very skeptically. ISTJ's can analyze large amounts of data expertly. When given time to reflect, they make buying decisions that are generally responsible, cost-effective, and good. ISTJ's will seldom make mistakes about facts.

**WEAKNESSES:** They like poring over data privately and sometimes appear aloof to salespeople. If they are in positions that require meetings, make sure you meet with them early in the day, or late, after everyone else has gone home.

**SALEBUSTERS:** Cold calls at "inappropriate" times (when they want to concentrate, which is usually the case). ISTJ's dislike poorly organized and presented proposals, and non-traditional ideas, especially ones that don't have factual support.

**HOW TO SELL TO THE ISTJ:** Prepare highly detailed, well-supported, organized, and neat proposals for them and send the proposals to the ISTJ before the meeting. This gives them time to analyze it privately, so they'll understand and appreciate your proposal fully. Schedule meetings well in advance. They'll view unsolicited phone calls and unscheduled meetings as unwelcome interruptions.

When meeting ISTJ's, give them time to speak. Make sure that the meeting doesn't run unnecessarily long.

# ISTP

| | |
|---|---|
| Dominant | Thinking |
| Secondary | Sensing |
| Tertiary | Intuitive |
| Inferior | Feeling |

**ISTP OCCUPATIONS:** military personnel, farmer, mechanic, engineer, dental hygienist, programmer.

**STRENGTHS:** ISTP's are excellent troubleshooters. They make excellent spontaneous decisions and respond quickly and correctly in the middle of a crisis. Some of the greatest generals were ISTP's because of the ISTP's excellent ability to analyze information and act spontaneously.

**WEAKNESSES:** They can become bored in non-crisis situations and may neglect people's feelings or new possibilities.

**SALEBUSTERS:** A long, drawn-out, tedious business cycle will tend to bore the ISTP and lose his or her interest. Having a large meeting or talking about theory won't work well.

**HOW TO SELL TO THE ISTP:** If your product would help solve a crisis, there's likely to be a short buying cycle. Send the ISTP a copy of your proposal detailing immediate benefit. Present your information neatly and logically.

# ISFJ

**Dominant** **Sensing**
Secondary Feeling
Tertiary Thinking
Inferior Intuitive

ISFJ OCCUPATIONS: nurse, teacher, librarian, physician, middle manager, secretary.

STRENGTHS: ISFJ's like traditional jobs and working in situations where they are of help to others. They have great organizational skills, but do not like to be confined to organizational and factual analysis. Unlike ISTJ's, ISFJ's tend not to gravitate toward upper management. They prefer working for someone else in a support position. ISFJ's greatest strength is analyzing facts in a personal way. Because of their ISJ traits, they have the keen ability to analyze information and their auxiliary Feeling trait helps them relate the data to human terms.

WEAKNESSES: ISFJ's inferior function is Intuitive. Although their goal is developing solutions that people like, they have difficulty considering ideas that are nontraditional.

SALEBUSTERS: ISFJ's won't respond well to "cold-hearted" presentations or "way out" ideas. They could also be easily overwhelmed by Extroverted presentations, especially if the presentation is theoretical, not factual, in nature.

HOW TO SELL TO THE ISFJ: Before a meeting, give the ISFJ a detailed proposal to read that 1) shows the practical benefit of your solution and, 2) includes customer references that they can call to insure that others who are affected by your solution will be satisfied with it.

# ISFP

**Dominant** **Feeling**
Secondary Sensing
Third Intuitive
Inferior Thinking

ISFP OCCUPATIONS: stock clerk, surveyor, mechanic, dental assistant, nurse, secretary.

STRENGTHS: ISFP's like harmonious environments and feel that people should enjoy their work. They'll buy products that are people-oriented and practical.

**WEAKNESSES:** ISFP's will notice things, but not mention them if it might cause a conflict. They won't be easily swayed by analytical arguments.

**SALEBUSTERS:** ISFP's don't like to buy products that will make people anxious in their work. Salespeople shouldn't overwhelm ISFP's with theoretical, or new, ideas or have large, disruptive meetings with them.

**HOW TO SELL TO THE ISFP:** Prepare an attractive presentation in advance and show a written copy of it to the ISFP. Show within the presentation practical ways to increase harmony immediately.

# INFJ

| | |
|---|---|
| **Dominant** | **Intuitive** |
| Secondary | Feeling |
| Tertiary | Thinking |
| Inferior | Sensing |

**INFJ OCCUPATIONS:** cleric, teacher, social worker, librarian, scientist.

**STRENGTHS:** INFJ's are very good at promoting harmony within a group. Their dominant Intuitive function allows them to explore several possibilities if they are presented to them. INFJ's are excellent at taking ideas and synthesizing them, and making plans happen.

**WEAKNESSES:** INFJ's don't like to be overwhelmed with details and impersonal analysis. This is especially true when there isn't a plan for implementation, or when they aren't given time to reflect privately.

**SALEBUSTERS:** Show-stoppers with the INFJ include focusing on details and excluding the human element in a buying decision. Salespeople not having specific plans or being too analytical will not be effective with an INFJ.

**HOW TO SELL TO THE INFJ:** Show the INFJ your proposal beforehand, and focus on the idea that people will be benefited quickly.

# INFP

| | |
|---|---|
| **Dominant** | **Feeling** |
| Secondary | Intuitive |
| Tertiary | Sensing |
| Inferior | Thinking |

**INFP OCCUPATIONS:** psychiatrist, editor, journalist, teacher, social worker.

**STRENGTHS:** INFP's are excellent at team building and creating group harmony. They tend to be idealistic and not very materialistic. They are the most careful decisionmakers of any type, and they will carefully debate alternatives internally until a decision can be made that will be good for all. They like buying things that will please people and developing strategies for easy and workable change. INFP's tend to have excellent ideas, but their Introverted nature means that you may have to ask them outright for their opinions on matters.

**WEAKNESSES:** INFP's tend to ignore the negative consequences of not making a decision, especially when there are people emotionally involved in it. They will not feel comfortable buying things relating to the Feeling function unless they are sure the people they're buying for will like what they have bought.

**SALEBUSTERS:** Criticism, rushing a decision, too much Extroverted enthusiasm, and ignoring the feelings of people involved in a decision.

**HOW TO SELL TO THE INFP:** Find out quickly if the decision relates to their dominant function, Feeling. If it does, make sure that all involved are happy. Work out, with them, possibilities for making everyone comfortable with the decision. If the sale doesn't relate to their dominant Feeling function, they are likely to make their decisions quickly.

Don't bog the INFP down with details. Send them information to review before any meeting. Make meetings short, and make sure they're scheduled well in advance.

INFP's tend to take impersonal comments as personal criticism. If your solution has negative consequences, don't brush them off.

# INTJ

| | |
|---|---|
| **Dominant** | **Intuitive** |
| Secondary | Thinking |
| Tertiary | Feeling |
| Inferior | Sensing |

**INTJ OCCUPATIONS:** attorney, scientist, researchers, programmer, photographer, manager.

**STRENGTHS:** INTJ's grasp new ideas quickly and easily. They are very good at developing plans for small groups. Both INTJ's and ENTJ's are excellent at understanding ideas, but INTJ's are more likely to lead people to their goals by example and tend to be more autonomous than ENTJ's.

**WEAKNESSES:** They don't want presentations rich in detail, even when buying products or services that require that detail. Sometimes INTJ's are so good at analytical reasoning that they can "reason out" the people involved in a decision.

**SALEBUSTERS:** Focusing in on details. Too much emphasis placed on non-analytical, emotional arguments. Not allowing time for the Introverted thought process to take place.

**HOW TO SELL TO THE INTJ:** Prepare presentations in advance. Send your INTJ customer your conceptual ideas, and let them mull them over. Give them time to respond to questions during meetings. Make sure the solutions presented to the INTJ allow them to lead, but without too much public interaction.

## INTP

| | |
|---|---|
| **Dominant** | **Thinking** |
| Secondary | Intuitive |
| Tertiary | Sensing |
| Inferior | Feeling |

**INTP OCCUPATIONS:** chemist, writer, artist, researcher, programmer, lawyer, scientist.

**STRENGTHS:** INTP's are good at creating systems, plans, or buildings. They have excellent problem solving abilities, but prefer to head off problems before they happen. Instead of being crisis managers, they tend to foresee problems and develop workable solutions logically.

**WEAKNESSES:** INTP's prefer theoretical problems, as opposed to immediate concerns, so tend to have extremely long buying cycles.

**SALEBUSTERS:** INTP's don't like presentations focused on practicality, emotion, or with the pressure of strict time frames. They much prefer being in low-stress environments where productivity isn't measured in the amount of work completed.

**HOW TO SELL TO THE INTP:** Send them proposals that focus on logical and objective reasoning covering theoretical possibilities. Plan for a long buying cycle that eventually will come through.

# Sensing types

|  | **With Thinking** | **With Feeling** |
|---|---|---|

**Introverts**

**Judging types**

### ISTJ
I Mull decisions privately
S Look for practicality
T Do logical analysis
J Decide on time deadline

### ISFJ
I Mull decisions privately
S Look for practicality
F Do human analysis
J Decide on time deadline

**Perceiving types**

### ISTP
I Mull decisions privately
S Look for practicality
T Do logical analysis
P Decide on event deadline

### ISFP
I Mull decisions privately
S Look for practicality
F Do human analysis
P Decide on event deadline

**Extroverts**

**Perceiving types**

### ESTP
E Verbalize thoughts
S Look for practicality
T Do logical analysis
P Decide on event deadline

### ESFP
E Verbalize thoughts
S Look for practicality
F Do human analysis
P Decide on event deadline

**Judging types**

### ESTJ
E Verbalize thoughts
S Look for practicality
T Do logical analysis
J Decide on time deadline

### ESFJ
E Verbalize thoughts
S Look for practicality
F Do human analysis
J Decide on time deadline

*Table of behavioral traits*

# Intuitive types

| With Feeling | With Thinking |
|---|---|

**Introverts**

**Judging types**

### INFJ

I  Mull decisions privately

N  Look for possibilities

F  Do a human analysis

J  Decide on time deadline

### INTJ

I  Mull decisions privately

N  Look for possibilities

T  Do logical analysis

J  Decide on time deadline

**Perceiving types**

### INFP

I  Mull decisions privately

N  Look for possibilities

F  Do a human analysis

P  Decide on event deadline

### INTP

I  Mull decisions privately

N  Look for possibilities

T  Do logical analysis

P  Decide on event deadline

**Extroverts**

**Perceiving types**

### ENFP

E  Verbalize thoughts

N  Look for possibilities

F  Do human analysis

P  Decide on event deadline

### ENTP

E  Verbalize thoughts

N  Look for possibilities

T  Do logical analysis

P  Decide on event deadline

**Judging types**

### ENFJ

E  Verbalize thoughts

N  Look for possibilities

F  Do human analysis

J  Decide on time deadline

### ENTJ

E  Verbalize thoughts

N  Look for possibilities

T  Do logical analysis

J  Decide on time deadline

# Conclusion

Sell to every customer's dominant function, and avoid selling to his inferior function. Perceiving types will set up an event schedule, and won't buy until their dominant function has been appeased.

When you know what a customer's personality type is, use Personality Selling to focus on the customer's strengths, while avoiding salebusters.

# Chapter 9
# CONSULTATIVE SELLING AND ACCOUNT MANAGEMENT

The goal of sales is to get repeat business because selling "onesy-twosies" is time consuming. Locating a prospect, determining personality, establishing credibility, qualifying, and so on, tend to take up an increasing amount of time if all your sales are first sales. You have to repeat the sales process from the beginning each time you sell something.

With repeat sales, you'll get to concentrate your efforts on finding solutions, instead of establishing credibility. You'll get easy business, called "bluebirds," sales you didn't work for that just drop in your lap because you're their rep.

## The Key Is Acting like a Consultant

The key to account management is in acting like a consultant. You sell consultatively when you deal with customers as if they were paying you for your service. You make recommendations independent of the commission you'll earn on the sale. People generally hire consultants to make sure they get right solutions at fair prices. Since they aren't on commission, consultants are free to make independent choices and their expertise will insure that the customer is getting a good deal. People use consultative salespeople to get the same level of expertise. Customers pay you indirectly by giving you their business, instead of paying you a consulting fee. The relationship between the customer and the consultative salesperson is the same as the relationship between a customer and a consultant.

## Win–Win Selling

The basis of consultative selling is a "win–win" strategy. Simply put, win–win means that you win by making money and the client wins by getting what he needs. There are four possible outcomes to every sale. They are:

| | Salesperson | Customer |
|---|---|---|
| **WIN–WIN** | WINS | WINS |
| **WIN–LOSE** | WINS | LOSES |
| **LOSE–WIN** | LOSES | WINS |
| **LOSE–LOSE** | LOSES | LOSES |

One rep asked during a seminar how he could sell win–win and still make quota. He worked in a high-pressure retail job where performance was measured on how few customers got away. His manager felt that if a customer left without buying, that customer wouldn't be back, and the sale would be lost. (See chapter 4 for the reasons this line of reasoning is faulty.) This rep was forced to practice the "tell 'em everything" school of selling. Because his store has a slew of unhappy customers, he didn't get many repeat or referral sales.

His lack of referral sales is understandable because although "winning" by "taking" customers may get him through the quarter, it will come back to haunt him. Selling win–lose (where the rep wins and the customer loses) doesn't always mean being a con artist who blatantly rips off customers. It can be, and it usually is, more subtle, as in the following scenario:

## Why Win–Lose Selling Doesn't Work

Chris sells lawn and garden equipment at The Garden Outlet. A customer named Sheila comes in, says she wants a new gas grill and explains her needs. A Grillmaster 500 catches her eye. It sells for $499 and needs assembly. Though he knows the smaller, preassembled Grillmaster 200, at $199, is big enough for her, Chris sees this as an impulse purchase and proceeds to sell her on the 500, which needs assembly.

He tells her, "If you buy the 500 now, you'll probably have it ready by dinner time." Chris knows the grill is difficult to assemble but reasons that, since he said "probably," he's in the clear because he made no explicit promise.

Sheila buys the grill and gets the tank filled with propane on the way home. There, she tries to assemble the grill. After several hours, she gives up and cooks her supper, a thick steak, on top of the stove.

The next day, when Sheila tries to return the grill, Chris says the store can't take it back because the tank's been filled. Sheila then notices the preassembled 200 and realizes that Chris sold her on the wrong product.

Unable to use the grill, Sheila complains to the president of The Garden Outlet. Her complaints filter down to Chris's boss, Ann Davidson. Ann offers Sheila free assembly and a $300 merchandise credit.

In return, Sheila agrees not to sue, but she tells everyone how unreasonable The Garden Outlet's return policy is and how unhappy she is with Chris.

## Why Win—Win Selling Does Work

This is how Chris should have sold to Sheila:

> "The Grillmaster 500 is too big for your needs, and it's impossible to assemble. The 200 is the right size, and you can use it right away."

Sheila would have bought the 200, and every time someone came over for a barbecue she'd mention where she bought the grill and recommend that her friends buy one, too.

Chris would have made more money with repeat and referral sales than he did by steering Sheila toward a product that she didn't need. He would have made more with "blue birds" by selling win—win and using Personality Selling.

## When You Lose, Nobody Wins

Your other responsibility, as a consultant, is not to set up sales where you lose and the customer wins. Here's an example:

> You've had a long day. Lisa, who bought a VCR at the lowest possible price and with the understanding that installation wasn't included, has called several times. You warned her that installation would be difficult. As you leave, Lisa calls again. You tell the receptionist to say you've already left. You know she won't buy anything else from you, but you're secretly relieved.

Lose—win eventually degrades to lose—lose because the losing parties will do what they can to "even the score." Every rep has had a customer like Lisa. Lisa is a hostile-aggressive and thinks she can have her low price and installation too.[22] (Chapter 10, "Selling to Difficult Customers," gives strategies for spotting and coping with the hostile-aggressive customer and avoiding lose—win or lose—lose situations.)

Let's compare Lisa to Diane, one of your best repeat customers.

> Diane bought the same VCR at a higher price. You were both happy with the price that didn't include installation, because you both thought installation would be easy, which it wasn't.

Diane calls at the end of the day. Instead of avoiding her, you talk her through the process of installing the VCR, taking as long as it takes.

Diane won because she has her VCR working. You won because you got a fair commission and a happy customer. Although you spent a little extra time on support, she'll remember the extra service and always buy from you despite sales and promotions that your competitors run.

# What If They *Want* You to Lose?

What do you do when customers insist on their winning and your losing?

## Explain the Benefits of Win—Win

If customers are seeking a lose–win sale, explain the mutual benefit of a win–win relationship to them. For example, let's say your competitor has priced a stereo system so low that if you matched the price you would make little money on the deal. Your customer, Stewart Lincoln, insists that you match the price. What do you do? Here's an example:

> "Mr. Lincoln, we don't have the highest prices in town or the lowest prices either. I wouldn't want to sell you my product at that [low] price because I couldn't support you."

If Stewart says he doesn't want support and is looking for the lowest price for a commodity item, say,

> "If someone told you that the product won't need support, that just isn't so. Selling to you without being able to support you would be a disservice. If we made money and you got bad service, you'd lose on the sale. If you got a great price and we lost money, we would lose. I propose a sale where both win."

## Respond in Terms Customers Understand

If Stewart persists, respond in terms he understands.

> **SALESPERSON:** You sell televisions, right? Do you have the lowest prices in town?
> **STEWART:** No. There's a mail order firm that sells most of my brands.

Your goal is to show Stewart that having the lowest prices isn't always best for the customer or the store. You'll do this by explaining to Stewart that his reasons for not having the lowest prices are the same as yours.

**SALESPERSON:** I bet they do it a lot cheaper.

**STEWART:** Yes, but they don't include warranty service.

**SALESPERSON:** Would you make money selling TV's at the price the mail order company does while still offering warranty service?

This question is on the verge of being an insincere question, because you are sure that the answer is going to be no.

**STEWART:** No. I'd lose on each sale.

**SALESPERSON:** So would we. That's why we, like you, can't afford to make sales at the lowest price.

Now Stewart understands your issues in terms he can relate to. Your customers want your products because what you sell fills a need. When you sell to them as their consultant, you're doing them a service.

# Steps to Being a Consultative Salesperson

1. **Discover the customers' needs.** Use your expertise to provide customers with information about the pros and cons of several different solutions.
2. **Forget about commission.** Make your recommendation based on what's best for the customer, not which solution has the higher margin. (Customers often underestimate the size or scope of purchases, so salespeople who sell consultatively often sell more, not less, although selling more isn't the goal.)
3. **Find areas of common interest.** In the case above, Stewart wanted to buy a stereo that was the best value, while you wanted to sell a stereo at a fair price. You had a common interest that you can talk about—getting Stewart the best stereo for his money.
4. **Tell the customer you want to sell win–win.** When the customer knows you've got his best interests in mind, he'll have your best interests in mind, too.
5. **Offer a guarantee.** If your solution doesn't work as you thought it would, don't let your customer swing in the wind. Take the product back and start looking for different solutions. The effort it takes starting from scratch is often less than the effort it takes to get a "bad solution" up and running. The confidence your customer will have in you in the future will be worth the price of the return.

# How to Get Repeat Sales

A happy customer is like gold. When you give good service and support, people will be happy to be a reference and to provide you with leads. If you ask them in an adult, professional manner, they'll be happy to rack their brains as they think of people for you to call. Honesty will pay big dividends:

> **SALESPERSON:** Craig, all of my current customers are all set. I need to get some new accounts. Do you know of anyone who I could call?
> **CRAIG:** Come to think of it, why don't you call my neighbor Chris. He's the operations manager for Bridge Street Welding. You could also call . . .

If year-end is coming and you need to make some sales to be in "The President's Club," or your company's equivalent, let your customers know. If you've done your customers favors over the year, they'll return the favors by pushing up a few orders so you'll "make your numbers."

# Don't Scam Your Customers

There are thousands of scams used by unscrupulous salespeople to weasel out the names and phone numbers of their customers' friends. Here's how a scam would work involving Joe, a high-pressure insurance salesman:

> **JOE:** I really appreciate your buying the life insurance. It seems like everyone today is expecting a baby.
> **TOM:** I know. My friends Jim and Michelle Irvine are having a baby in a couple of months.

Joe then looks up Jim and Michelle's phone number and pretends that Tom gave him a reference. He calls up Jim and Michelle, tells them Tom told him to call, and then starts his pitch. Usually Jim or Michelle will listen for a while because they think their friend, Tom, gave the reference. However, they usually won't buy anything.

If the scam does work and Jim and Michelle do buy insurance, eventually the scam will come out and Jim, Michelle, and Tom will feel cheated and not want to deal with Joe.

# Getting References Without Scams

In most cities, the biggest buildings belong to insurance companies. That would lead one to believe, rightfully so, that most insurance salespeople are not scam artists like Joe. You can do all the reference selling you want; just be honest with the customer.

Anytime you deal with someone, be up front about your intentions. This is how an insurance salesperson named Gail asked Tom for a reference:

> **GAIL:** Tom, even though people sometimes need additional insurance when they get married or have a baby, many people are apprehensive when insurance salespeople call them. They don't like being cold-called, so I don't do it. If you know of anyone I could help, would you give them my card?
>
> **TOM:** Sure. In fact, my friends Jim and Michelle are expecting a baby. I'll have them call you.

Gail asks all her customers for references and gets as many qualified leads as she can handle. She doesn't need to be surreptitious to get referrals. Using an honest approach, she sells much more than Joe does using a dishonest approach.

## Reference Selling Is Easier

The main reason why you do reference selling is that reference selling is easier than cold-calling selling. This is because people value the opinions of friends or colleagues whom they trust. You have to do much less work convincing a reference account you're good at your job if someone they respect tells them for you. When you're selling to a big account, you do a form of reference selling. In corporate sales, you constantly ask if there are any other departments that you could sell to.

## Account Management—Personality Selling Goes Long-Term

Account management is sustaining long-term win–win relationships and keeping customers happy with their choice of vendor, namely you. This way they'll make multiple purchases from you, often without consulting any other vendors.

## Corporate Personality Selling

Selling to businesses is often easier than selling to individuals because people find it easier spending the company's money and working from budgets. Individuals who are spending their own money obviously find it harder to part with. The larger the sale, the more the customer has to rely on his salesperson because often his job depends on the rep's knowledge, consultative skills, and responsiveness. This puts the rep and the decision maker in a mutually beneficial relationship. "No one ever got fired for buying IBM" is true because Big Blue doesn't let the customer down and always makes the decision maker look good.

It's well known that if IBM promises a solution will work and unforeseen problems creep up, IBM will spend whatever money is necessary and make every effort to make the solution work as promised. If a data processing manager tells his boss that an IBM product will, for instance, process payroll, the DP manager won't need to worry that IBM won't come through.

Successful corporate Personality Selling starts by establishing credibility in the customer's eyes. Your ability to handle a large account continues with guarantees that your solutions will work, and finishes with effective reference selling. Using these three ideas as a foundation, there are several steps, listed below, that insure successful corporate sales and account management.

**STEP 1: Find out where the power bases are.** Use Personality Selling to develop a relationship with the "powers that be." Once you've sold the people in charge, start selling to the people below them:

> "Fred Mangin, the VP of operations, wanted me to talk to you about some projects you're working on to see if I could be of any help."

You won't always be able to start with upper management in a company. Lee Iacocca doesn't have the time to speak with every salesperson who wants to sell to Chrysler. Sometimes you'll have to start low in the company, and work your way up. Sometimes a low-level manager will need a relatively small item. This can be your entree to the higher-level decision makers. You could say, "When I deliver the toner, could you introduce me to the operations manager? I'd like to tell him about some other things we can do."

**STEP 2: Look the part of the executive.** If your physical appearance suggests you're the kind of salesperson who is used to getting big accounts, you'll often get them. *Dress for Success*, by John T. Molloy, contains specific information on what to wear, but looking like an IBM salesperson is always a safe bet. This means navy blue or gray suit (not polyester), white shirt (laundered), and red tie for salesmen and comparatively conservative dress for saleswomen. Dressing like this may be boring to some people, but it will set an image designed to build confidence in companies that are looking to spend thousands, or millions, of dollars.

**STEP 3: Personality Sell.** Get to know the personalities of people in the corporation and the corporate personality itself. Though you'll be dealing in multiple sales cycles with several different departments selling large volumes, follow the principles in chapters 1–6.

**STEP 4: Don't take on too many accounts.** Make sure you have only as many accounts as you can fully support. Many successful reps only have one big account, but that one account buys regularly.

## Maintaining the Account

Maintaining a big account for a long time takes a great deal of work. You'll have several sales cycles working simultaneously for different solutions because you'll be selling to many departments at once. If you sell to an account long enough, your customers will change management or purchasing staff. This means that sometimes you'll have to start the sales process over again with the new guard right from the start, establishing credibility. An advantage is that you'll have a track record with the company that your competitors won't have—use it to your advantage.

Another reality of long-term account maintenance is that, during lulls in the business cycle, accounts are still going to need support—even when their level of purchasing is lower than usual.

## Long-Term Relationships Are Complex

Long-term relationships are complex and sales is no exception. Customers, being human, will eventually get frustrated dealing with a company, or even you, at times. Long-term sales relationships survive because of you, not your employer. Sales is unique in that your boss pays you, but you're working for the customer. An old sales adage says, "Sell yourself first, your company second, and your products third." If what you're selling is you, customers will put up with a little grief from your company. If you occasionally make a mistake, customers will overlook it. People are generally tolerant of honest mistakes when they know salespeople work hard for them.

# Cognitive Dissonance

Customers often won't notice or will overlook mistakes because of a phenomenon called cognitive dissonance. If they have bought from you in the past and have been happy with the service you provided, they will continue to feel that way partly because of dissonance. Cognitive dissonance causes people to look on the good side of things. It works like this: If a couple sees a Broadway show and spends three hundred dollars on the tickets, parking, and dinner, they would feel as if they wasted their money if the show was bad. They want to feel good about going to the show. So if the show wasn't that good, instead of thinking of reasons they *didn't* like it, they'll think of reasons they *did* like it. If they saw the same show on television, their reviews might be much more negative because the show was free. They had no money "invested" in the show to cause dissonance.

People expect to enjoy *Phantom of the Opera* before they see it because of its great reviews. They want to like it before it starts. When people are in a positive mind frame, dissonance ensures their enjoyment of the show. When people plan to like something, they usually do. In this way, a strong referral from a customer to a trusted friend (see above) works because the friend expects to like you before actually meeting you.

Likewise, customers invest much work in choosing you as their vendor and purchasing your products as their solution. Dissonance works in your favor because they'll want to feel good about their choices and will look for the positive things in what you do and what you sell.

# Ask a Favor

Another psychological phenomenon that works for salespeople is that, when someone does you a favor, they are more likely to have a positive feeling toward you. Some salespeople don't want to "put customers out" by asking customers for favors. Done in moderation, however, customers will actually like the reps they do things for more than the reps they don't do things for. Why? Many psychologists believe that in doing a favor for someone, we tend to think, "I must like this person, or else I wouldn't be doing this for them."

# Think Long-Term

Cognitive dissonance and good support will excuse the occasional screw-up (even big ones). Continued bad support will erode dissonance and not save reps who mistreat their accounts. Dissonance isn't a cure-all for long-term poor service. Servicing an account that's buying a lot is easy. Many customers get irritated when there's a drop-off in a salesperson's service during lean purchasing periods.

Most annual reports have a graph that shows earnings. The graph is usually an upward-sloping jagged line. Dips in revenue cause the jags. These dips have many causes: seasonal fluctuation, interest rates, inflation, unemployment. One of the fallouts of a revenue drop is that purchasing slows down temporarily. This means there will be periods when you'll spend precious time doing support for a few sales. The vast majority of customers know this and won't abuse your time. Most will return your efforts with "bluebirds" and loyalty. For my big accounts, I've spent days researching special items like printer wheels that cost ten dollars each and had commissions of only twenty-five cents. Those same customers gave me hundred-thousand-dollar orders without putting the orders to bid or expecting special discounts.

Managing big, loyal accounts is a good job to have but one that requires much effort.

## What About a Drop in Volume?

A drop in volume bothers some sales managers, who may pressure you to give the account less attention and to find other business. If this is the case, take your manager in to see the account, so the decision makers themselves can tell your boss business will be picking up. That will usually do the trick because your manager will see the long-term benefits of keeping the account and their need of support. He'll cut you some slack at month's end if you are a little short of quota.

## Sometimes Companies Change Vendors

Sometimes companies give so little support to their reps that customers have to change vendors. This may happen so quickly that salespeople can't react, and they lose the account. Insulation Supply Company, where a sales rep named Rachel works, couldn't order enough inventory because of accounts receivable problems. Pam, the purchasing agent for Murphy Construction, thinks Rachel is a top-notch salesperson, but she needs to find another vendor.

> **PAM:** Rachel, I appreciate all you've done for us. The backorders from Insulation Supply are just too long. As much as I

like dealing with you, I cannot run a ten-million-dollar construction company when I'm always behind due to back orders of your products.

## Sow the Seeds Early—Then React

The secret to holding on to an account is to find out customers are dissatisfied as quickly as possible. That way, you and your manager can do something to remedy the problem. Early in the relationship, ask customers to let you know whenever they are dissatisfied with you, your service, or your company:

> "I'm going to do my best to support you. If I should fall down at any time, let me know, so I can address the issues. This is how I earn my living and I know customers sometimes don't tell salespeople they're not happy, they just cut them off. I want you to tell me. I'm here for the long run and two-way communication is essential."

Giving customers "permission" to tell you they're not happy allows them to express their gripes and allows you to focus on the issues before they become serious. Unhappy customers are often satisfied with their salesperson, but dissatisfied with the sales rep's organization. If you need more support from your company, involve your manager, his manager, and so on. Your managers won't want to lose the account either, and will give you the help you need. If Pam (above) had told Rachel about her concerns before the back-order situation became critical, Rachel could have brought in her boss, Jenny, to save the account.

> **PAM:** We are experiencing critical delays in insulation from your company. If I don't have all my orders filled in a week, I'm going to have to cancel them and buy from some place else.
> **JENNY:** I understand your concern and we'll have all the orders filled in time. We've been having some inventory problems because of accounts receivable, but I'll see that the money gets released today so we can place your order with our supplier.
> **PAM:** Rachel has given us great service over the last year. If cash flow's the only issue, in return for all your company has done for us in times of crisis, I'd be happy to pre-pay these orders.

**JENNY:** In that case, you'll have the materials in two days. Thank you.

Since Rachel gave Pam permission to make her gripes known, the crisis was averted. Jenny and Pam could negotiate a win–win solution. Like the proverbial snowball down the mountain, the sooner problems are dealt with, the quicker and easier solutions often are.

# Other Reps Will Want Your "Peach"

It's a natural tendency to want to "cruise on reputation" with accounts that are deliriously happy with you. The fact is that the accounts you won with hard work and talent, other salespeople will want to take. Make sure not to let hard-earned accounts slip away by getting careless. Customers will be loyal and remember all the times you went "above and beyond" for them. They'll excuse the occasional lapse in service or blunder but not consistently poor or not much more than mediocre performance. To insure keeping your accounts, remember all the things you did to get the business in the first place, and continue doing those things.

# Deliver the Solution

The sale isn't over until you deliver. In the perfect world, products are always in stock, and you can deliver what you promised when you promised. The real world has back orders and customers who ponder whether or not they should buy something for months, only to want it yesterday once they decide. Perceiving customers will generally be patient. Judging customers, with delivery deadlines elapsed, won't wait.

Don't allow Judging types to set deadlines when product is scarce. If there's a delay, call customers (especially Judging types) regularly so they don't feel forgotten.

If unforeseen problems crop up that prevent delivery, negotiate alternatives to the initial solution with the customer. Jack Wilson, a landscaper, ordered a lawn mower early in the spring that, weeks later, hasn't been delivered.

**SALESPERSON:** The lawn mower you bought is back ordered. I know this is your busy season. I can either get you a similar model made by Lawncare, or I can loan you a more expensive model until yours comes in. Are either of these alternatives acceptable?

**JACK:** If you can get me the Lawncare model by this week-end, fine. If not, I'll need the loaner.

Jack won't remember you didn't deliver the mower he ordered. He will remember that you solved his problem, and you were willing to be flexible. In return, he'll be flexible with you, and he'll give you future business.

# Call the Next Day

Anytime you sell a product or service, call soon after it is delivered to make sure everything's okay. This has a triple benefit. First, most problems with set-up, installation, or training happen within the first 48 hours after delivery. Your calling and fixing the problem will often steer the customers in the right direction.

Second, during the sales cycle you promised the customer superior support, and told them you wouldn't forget them after the sale was made. Your calling is definitive proof that you were truthful.

Third, the consultative service you provided before the sale and the follow-up phone calls you've made after the sale have earned you the right to ask them to be a reference. You can also ask customers if they know any prospects for you to call.

# Don't Forget to Write

It's always a good idea to send customers a short letter thanking them for their business. Make sure the letter is sincere and not a canned speech. Letters like:

> I'd like to thank you for buying from Hudson Controls, New Hampshire's leader in service and support. You'll find you'll be happy with your purchase. Thanks for being another satisfied Hudson customer.

aren't sincere, and the recipients know it. Not only will you fail to win any points with the customer, you'll have them wondering why you bothered writing.

A sincere letter will work wonders. It doesn't have to be long or a literary masterpiece:

> Thank you for buying your switching equipment from me and Hudson Controls. Every customer is important to me, so if you have any questions, feel free to call me at any time.

Customers appreciate this kind of letter and get the "warm and cushy feeling" that you want them to have.

# Conclusion

The only deals that will work long term are deals in which both parties win. Make sure that every deal you enter is win–win. Taking customers for a bath or letting customers gouge you will come back to haunt you. Follow these steps to be a consultative salesperson:

STEP 1: Discover customers' needs.

STEP 2: Forget about commission.

STEP 3: Find areas of common interest.

STEP 4: Tell the customer you want to sell win–win.

STEP 5: Offer a guarantee.

Use the same techniques to get big accounts as you do with smaller ones. Take the long view of an account; think like an account manager. Customers will remember that your support continued during slow periods, and they will reward you with loyalty. Follow these steps to be a successful account manager:

STEP 1: Find out where the power bases are. (Sometimes you'll have to start low and work your way up the company.)

STEP 2: Look the part of the executive.

STEP 3: Personality Sell.

STEP 4: Don't take on too many accounts.

# Chapter 10
# SELLING TO DIFFICULT CUSTOMERS

Most salespeople tend to avoid difficult customers and forfeit their business. When salespeople deal with difficult customers, it's usually because the customer buys so much that salespeople tolerate the customer's abusive behavior. This is known as economic "greenmail." In this situation long term, salespeople will become miserable doing their job, or tend to avoid all contact with the difficult customer. Eventually, they give up the difficult customer's business as the difficult customer, invariably, becomes even more difficult.

This chapter offers an alternative to avoidance or misery. It provides strategies for dealing with difficult people, explaining the causes of the behavior. Armed with the causes of the problem, and a strategy for the cure, you will be able to deal with difficult behaviors unemotionally and effectively. The description of the behaviors and strategies for coping were developed using ideas from the psychological field of Transactional Analysis and from the book *Coping with Difficult People* by Robert Bramson, Ph.D.[23]

## Difficult Customers

Customers who abuse or waste salespeople's time are known as difficult customers. All salespeople have had the misfortune of having a customer who was ornery, mean, or abusive. Difficult people can make sales, or any job, stressful. Fortunately, most customers are pleasant, easy to deal with, and only occasionally difficult. These strategies for dealing with difficult people will only have to be used with a small percentage of your customers.

### Power Plays

In hockey, a team is penalized by having a player put in the penalty box. This gives the other team a few minutes when they have an "extra" player on the ice. This added advantage is called a power play. Usually the team that has a power play scores because they have the upper hand during the penalty. In psychology, when one person has the upper hand over someone else, it's also called a power play. There are three types of power plays: one-up, one-down and even.[24]

## One-Up Power Plays

One-up power occurs when one party can bully the other party. The classic example of one-up power is a prison guard who has the power to shoot inmates who don't do what he says.

Vendors only have one-up power if they're monopolies. The phone company used to be a non-regulated monopoly. Ma Bell had one-up power and could coerce people by threatening to turn off phone service. Today, government regulation protects customers against monopolistic companies exerting one-up power over customers.

Customers, in theory, do have one-up power over salespeople because they are free to take their business away. Like the hockey team that has more players on the ice, the customer abusing a one-up power position will attempt to get what he wants using force.

> **DIFFICULT CUSTOMER:** If you send me any more defective products, I'll cancel the volume purchase contract I have with you immediately.

Usually companies are dependant on their vendors to a greater or lessor degree, so their power is not absolute.

> **CUSTOMER:** The defective rate is much higher than I want. We need your products and you need our business, so tell your quality control team to be more careful before they ship.

## One-Down Power Plays

One-down power occurs when one party doesn't have the authority to exercise force over another. He uses guerrilla techniques and indirect methods to get what he wants. A five-year-old can't coerce his parents by force, but can get even with them by saying things he knows will get the parents arguing. In the example below, a woman uses one-down power to "get even" with a restaurant that treated her badly:

> Nancy Goode, a patron of a seafood restaurant called The Fish House had a badly prepared meal that the restaurant refused to take back.
> Nancy used her one-down power as customer to hurt the restaurant by complaining about the restaurant's service on radio talk shows, writing newspaper editorials, and telling all her friends not to eat at the restaurant.

People who are happy with a purchase tend to tell a few people about the purchase they made. People who are unhappy use their one-down power and tend to tell *thirty to fifty* people about the purchase they wish they had never made. Salespeople should never underestimate the one-down power of unhappy customers.

## Even-Power Plays

Even-power plays occur when neither party has the power to coerce the other blatantly, like a chess match when both players start with the same number of pieces. Even-power players try to outmaneuver opponents. They look for weaknesses and usually strike hard.

# Difficult People

Upcoming in this chapter, we will be looking at five types of difficult people salespeople often have to deal with: Sherman tanks, the super-agreeables, the know-it-all experts, and exploders.[25]

## The Occasionally Difficult

There's a difference between the chronically difficult and the occasionally difficult. Everyone is difficult at times. Occasionally difficult people become difficult temporarily when they're pushed beyond their limits (usually by the salesperson himself). The general strategy for handling them is to just let them vent their frustration, then move on, since the behavior will be acute, but short term.

## Chronically Difficult People

Chronically difficult people go through life leaving a wake of destruction behind them. They are constantly making the lives of other people, including the vendors who have to deal with them, difficult or miserable. Fortunately, difficult people can be dealt with using the techniques in this chapter. This leaves you with a management decision to make. Even when coping techniques are effective, if applying them is time-consuming, should you look to other accounts? This is a personal decision. If you could manage two non-difficult if smaller accounts and bring in a similar amount of business in the time it takes to manage one difficult one, by all means skip the difficult one.

Sometimes, however, customers buy so much that you decide you must deal with them despite their difficult and sometimes hostile dispositions. Here are some techniques that will make your life easier.

# The Customer Is *Not* Always Right

An old business adage states, "The customer is always right." Difficult customers interpret that saying to mean that spending money brings them divine infallibility, no matter how much they spend. I've seen people being abusive to sales clerks at McDonald's because their french fries were "lukewarm."

Frequently, difficult customers look down on salespeople and treat them like children who must be punished. Transactional Analysts (TA)[26] call this behavior acting like a "pig." These types of difficult people believe they're superior to salespeople and others and feel it is their right to be verbally abusive to people they see as "inferiors." "Pig" customers, needless to say, make salespeople's lives miserable.

# Talk with the Difficult Customer "Adult to Adult"

Psychologists say that when difficult people speak in an abusive manner toward people, it is like an adult reprimanding a little child. This verbal transaction is known as a "script" because the person being abused is expected to play the part of a penitent child and act like one, as if he or she were in a play. (Transactional Analysis psychologists label several types of scripts difficult people enjoy playing, and develop strategies[27] for dealing with people using such scripts.) Your job as a salesperson is to make the difficult customer understand that you're not interested in playing such a role in his "script" by speaking to him as an adult and not accepting, or returning, his abuse. You take control, and force the relationship to proceed on an adult–adult level. Here's an example:

> **"PIG" CUSTOMER:** I paid good money for these french fries and they're lukewarm. You're an incompetent boob.
> **SALESCLERK:** Don't speak to me like that. I won't accept it. (The salesclerk shouldn't address the issue of the fries until the customer deals with him on an adult level.)

> **RATIONAL CUSTOMER:** Could you please reheat these or give me some others?
> **SALESCLERK:** Sure.

People who view salespeople as inferiors will treat them as peers when salespeople force the relationship to proceed on an adult–adult level.

Here are specific strategies for dealing with different kinds of difficult customers.

## Sherman Tanks

The first type of difficult customer is the Sherman tank. The Sherman tank is a hostile, aggressive person who tries to threaten, roll over, and destroy everything in his path. Sherman tanks use their one-up power as customer to threaten salespeople far beyond what is acceptable in the normal course of business. They will demand from their rep service, support, and pricing beyond what is fair. They often control large budgets because, if they didn't, few people would bother dealing with them. Salespeople who kowtow to their obnoxious behavior because of their economic strength get drawn into their psychological script. The salesperson winds up on the losing end of a lose–win deal. (See chapter 9.) This situation involves a hostile aggressive known as the "Sherman tank."[28]

> **CUSTOMER:** Bill, the computer network you sold me still isn't working. When's your technician coming over to install it?
>
> **SALESPERSON:** When you bought the network you received a large discount because you said your technicians would install it.
>
> **CUSTOMER:** Well, they're too busy now, and I don't like seeing this equipment just sitting here. If no one comes by, I'll return the equipment and deal with a vendor that will install it and give them all my business.
>
> **SALESPERSON:** Sending our technicians now would incur expenses far ahead of revenues on the sales and we'd lose money.
>
> **CUSTOMER:** It's your decision. Take it or leave it.

This is an extreme but not uncommon case of a "pig" customer engaging in a one-up power play. It's a form of blackmail known as greenmail, threatening to take important business away from the salesperson. Salespeople often succumb to greenmail, but they cannot sustain receiving the unfair treatment. After a while the rep gives up the account, or his company goes out of business.

Typically, before dealing with the greenmailer, the salesperson has heard horror stories about the greenmailer, but thinks to himself, "How difficult could they be?"

He usually finds out quickly that he has gotten more than he bargained for and eventually stops doing business with the greenmailer.

After Sherman tanks greenmail every supplier, and no vendors want to deal with them, they start dealing fairly or are left with no suppliers. This type of customer routinely demands such large discounts and disproportionately large amounts of support that vendors are regularly forced out of business. These vendors do not realize, until it's too late that, although their revenues are high, they can't make up loss on volume. The example below shows how a Sherman tank tries to green-mail his supplier, along with how to cope with him.

**COPING WITH THE SHERMAN TANK:** First, meet with the customer in person. This will allow eye-contact and prevent premature closure of the meeting, easily done by the Sherman tank during a phone conversation.

> **SHERMAN TANK** (on the phone): Those are my conditions, take them or leave them. Listen, I've got another call. I've got to go. G'bye.

Explain that a healthy business relationship builds itself on a win–win strategy. Give examples of the consequences to him if his customers were to treat him with one-up power plays. Finally, focus on the issues. State the consequences to him of his causing vendors to lose and how win–lose relationships degenerate to lose–lose relationships. Develop a strategy for solving the customer's problem without giving in to threats or intimidation. Here is an example of how to cope with the Sherman tank:

> **SALESPERSON:** The list price for the equipment is $10,000. You received it for $5,000 because your technicians would install the system. Is this correct?
>
> **CUSTOMER:** Yes, but as I said before, they're too busy now and I need the system up and running immediately.
>
> **SALESPERSON:** I understand how you feel. Many customers buy networks and later need our technicians. How would you feel if one of your customers bought 2,000 pounds of meat and received a large discount because they said they would pick it up themselves and then came back and said they wanted to have you deliver the product at the same price? That would be a win–lose situation because your company would be losing money. The situation would eventually degrade to lose–lose because your company couldn't profitably do business with them.
>
> We are trying to develop a long-term relationship with your company. I understand that you need your network up and running quickly. Since our technicians are familiar with your system, we could start installing tomorrow. We can discount the technicians' services because of the volume of equipment purchased. If you sign this authorization, we'll start work for an additional $3,000.
>
> **CUSTOMER:** All right. But I need this running by the end of the week.

If the customer persists in demanding more than is fair, the rep should say he can't do business with him for the same reasons the customer wouldn't do business under similar conditions—it's a win–lose deal that will ultimately be lose–lose. The Sherman tank will respect that reasoning and usually acquiesce to fairness.

If the salesperson gives in, it guarantees repeated greenmail. When "pig" customers are allowed to engage in one-up power plays, the difficult behavior will worsen until the win–lose situation is so out of control that the salesperson bails out. Hoping the customer will become fair, or misinterpreting brief periods of adult–adult behavior as a change in character, is misplaced optimism. Sherman tanks become *more* demanding, not less, with each "victory."

If no amount of coping techniques are effective, the salesperson must decide whether the extra costs of greenmail are worth the benefit of having a big account. There are many big accounts and often the rep can make more by finding other accounts to deal with.

# The Super-Agreeable

The super-agreeable is the customer who "kills you with kindness." The super-agreeable avoids confrontations and conflict and will say anything, true or not, to keep people from getting upset. When the super-agreeable, for instance, has funding for a project fall through, he'll put off telling you because he knows you'll be disappointed.

## A Super-Agreeable Drain

The super-agreeable will be a greater drain on your paycheck than the hostile aggressive because the super-agreeable will be outwardly pleasant and the damage he is causing is subtle. You may not even realize you're selling to a difficult person. For any number of reasons, you don't get the sale, but the super-agreeable avoids telling you the "bad" news. He'll string you along, knowing you've lost the sale, telling you the project's "just about ready," or he needs a few more approvals, or he wants just a little more information.

> **SALESPERSON:** We have plenty of office dividers in stock to fill the order you need. Is the purchase order ready?
> **SUPER-AGREEABLE:** (whose boss has decided not to order for another year): The PO is just about ready. My boss is taking one final look at it. Could you get me the price if we got ten more sets?
> **SALESPERSON:** Sure.

## Perceiving Types Aren't Difficult

The super-agreeable's delaying shouldn't be confused with customers waiting until salespeople address their dominant function. Perceiving types are careful decision makers who wait for events to occur before they'll buy. They're not decision avoiders. If a Perceiving type hasn't bought because he's missing a critical piece of information, he's not being difficult. He'll buy when he gets the information. Perceiving types with dominant functions of Feeling and Intuition will be slowest because Intuitives tend to want to discover all the possibilities, and Feeling types will be interested in all human impact of the decision. When all three personality traits are present, in theory boundless amounts of data must be weighed. In business, the expectation to make "a decision" is great. If a customer is a slow decision maker, then bringing the customer to closure (which is necessary for the super-agreeable, since often a decision is already made) would be viewed by the Perceiving type as being rushed into a decision—something Perceiving types dislike.

COPING WITH THE SUPER-AGREEABLE Listen to the customer and focus on the issues as much as possible (see chapter 6). Find reasons why the super-agreeable is avoiding or delaying making a decision. If you feel the project is cancelled or delayed, give your customer "permission" to tell you the news,[29] using "us," or "we." Here are some examples:

> SALESPERSON: The quote's been out for three months now. Let's go over it again to make sure there's nothing we left out.

> SALESPERSON: I heard that several departments had cutbacks. Did our project get hit?

> SALESPERSON: I feel you still have some concerns about how the project will affect the office.
> CUSTOMER: Well, it's such a big change.
> SALESPERSON: Why don't we bring in a prototype and get feedback.

When the customer admits there is a problem:

> SALESPERSON: Why don't we scale down the project and take it one step at a time.

> SALESPERSON: Project delays are inevitable. I'm not going to close every sale and, most importantly, my time is precious. You're actually doing me less of a service by not telling

me when projects get cancelled because I could be spending time selling to someone else.

**CUSTOMER:** It looks as if I lost funding for the order. I've been trying to get the additional money in my budget, but I don't think I'll be able to.

**SALESPERSON:** Thanks for telling me.

The super-agreeable's biggest fear is disappointing you. If you are disappointed, don't show it. This will leave the door open for future business.

# Know-It-All Experts

The know-it-all expert is the customer who seems to know everything about everything. There are two types of know-it-all experts, and sales reps can play an important role in their scripts. The two types are the bulldozer (one who bullies others into accepting his opinion) and the balloon (the pseudo-expert). The know-it-all expert wants sales reps to play the part of "yes-man." A sales rep, who wants the know-it-all expert's business, quickly learns to agree with everything said, and be very impressed with the knowledge of the know-it-all expert.

The know-it-all expert will enjoy a comfortable relationship with a yes-man salesperson, but the relationship is based on the subservience of the salesperson, not on mutual respect and benefit. Also, if the know-it-all expert makes a poor decision, the rep will be blamed for not providing insight, even if insight was discouraged.

> **KNOW-IT-ALL EXPERT:** Why didn't you tell me that fire codes said the cable has to be specially coated?
>
> **SALESPERSON:** I tried, but you said you knew all the fire codes.

Know-it-all experts who are ultimate decision makers want yes-men and order-takers. Know-it-all experts who aren't final decision makers act as powerfully negative forces adding unnecessary confusion and uncertainty to the buying process.

## The Bulldozer

The first type of know-it-all expert is the bulldozer, who bullies others into agreeing (albeit outwardly) with his opinions. More than any other type of difficult person, the bulldozer views salespeople with condescension. Bulldozers get salespeople off balance in the salespeople's most vulnerable situation, group meetings. Salespeople speaking in front of a group cannot be made to look as if they don't know their business (chapter 2). Being argumentative or controversial toward a member of a group during a meeting never has a happy ending. Members of the group must show loyalty to co-workers or bosses present at the meeting, even if they know that their boss was the one being difficult. The bulldozer works like this: The rep asserts an idea or statement. The bulldozer makes a counter-assertion. If it is a major point and the salesperson says nothing, he or she will be viewed by some members of the group as incompetent or unknowledgeable—minimizing credibility. Yet, challenging the boss will force people to take sides, dividing the group, and ultimately swaying the group away from the rep.

**COPING WITH THE BULLDOZER:** Empathize with bulldozers and discover what they are getting at.

"I understand what you're saying. I've heard that idea before. Let's see if it would work in this situation."

This will inevitably lead to dismissal of the idea by the bulldozer himself because it will be apparent that his comment is unworkable. (Truly listen to the bulldozer's ideas and don't reject them out of hand because of their presentation, because some of the bulldozer's comments will be valid and useful.)

**ALLOW THE BULLDOZER TO SAVE FACE:** Your insightful questioning will show you as competent and knowing your business while allowing the bulldozer to save face. Ironically, the bulldozer is usually abusive to salespeople because he is threatened by the salesperson's knowledge. Salespeople who force their knowledge on the bulldozer will threaten the bulldozer even more, and the bulldozer will return an increased level of abusive behavior. Showing deference to the bulldozer (in an adult manner) will allow the bulldozer to appear competent and knowledgeable to his co-workers. If the bulldozer's idea is rejected, it will be because you both worked the idea through together and discovered it was unworkable, not because the bulldozer was ignorant. Too, the bulldozer can be seen as having "tested you" and your working it out means you "passed." In this example, the bulldozer has just accused Boris, a copier salesman, of trying to oversell him on the size of a copier. (Boris knows from previous meetings that the bulldozer is an ESTJ (Extroverted, Sensing, Thinking, Judging) type. Boris will appeal to the bulldozer's dominant function of Thinking by doing a logical analysis of his choice of copier.)

**BORIS:** What makes you think the copier I've proposed is too big?

**BULLDOZER:** The copier is too big because all you sales-people try to sell us too much.

**BORIS:** The copier I've proposed handles 1000–1500 copies per day. Let's see what your volume is. How many copies of reports do you do every day?

**BULLDOZER:** About 400 copies.

**BORIS:** How many miscellaneous copies do you do?

**BULLDOZER:** About 500 to 700.

**BORIS:** The reason I'm here is that the copier you have isn't keeping up with the volume. The data you've provided says that a copier that would handle 1000–1500 copies per day is a good one. Would you agree?

**BULLDOZER:** Yes. It's a good choice.

If the bulldozer sticks to his guns, it will become apparent he is a know-it-all expert to the other members of the group, who will reject the idea behind closed doors when you're not around. Leave the idea as a possibility and allow the bulldozer's own people to handle him later.

**BULLDOZER:** I don't care what that salesman says. He's trying to rip us off.

**JACK** (a co-worker after Boris has left): Boris has done a lot of work for us. His facts are solid and his choice is logical. I don't think he's trying to take us.

## The Balloon

The second type of know-it-all expert is the balloon, a pseudo-expert who seems to know everything about everything. In reality, the balloon can speak confidently about subjects he knows little or nothing about. Cliff from the television show "Cheers" is a balloon. Balloons are different from bulldozers in that balloons aren't malicious. They just honestly *believe* they are experts. They are often no more than an annoyance, but can manage to get meetings or sales cycles off track.

COPING WITH THE BALLOON: To cope with the balloon, carefully listen to the balloon and filter fact from fiction. This can be difficult because balloons seem confident and often have sound arguments, although they base their conclusions on incomplete or inaccurate data. In the following example, Ron is trying to sell VCR's to a bank chain for their conference centers. Kurt, a balloon, is throwing in his opinions about VCR's being radioactive, which they're not.

**KURT (THE BALLOON):** The VCR's you're proposing are a threat to the health of the employees because of their radioactive emissions.
**RON (THE SALESPERSON):** I've heard that concern before. There are a lot of people who've been misinformed that VCR's emit radiation. The fact is that some televisions emit low levels of radioactivity, which our monitors don't do.

Show deference since saving face is most important to the balloon. Use phrases like, "I've heard that before, but after research we found . . ." or "That's right, but there's more to it than that."

Assert yourself as an expert immediately. That way the balloon can show himself as an expert by agreeing with you, often citing verifiable sources like trade journals.

**BALLOON:** Ron is absolutely right about that. There was an article in *Consumer Reports* about VCR's, and what he's saying is correct.

# The Exploder

"The squeaky wheel gets the oil" is the rallying cry of the exploder. The exploder is the customer who rants, raves, and attacks the salesperson, whom he feels is inferior and needs to be "taught a lesson."

Usually these bursts of intense anger are short-lived and the customer will act in a reasonable manner after the explosion.

In the exploder's script, he plays a cross between a child having a temper tantrum and a parent teaching a child a lesson. His role is to humiliate the salesperson, while the salesperson's role is to listen quietly and feel contrite. It is the ultimate form of a positional conversation, in which the exploder's position is the only one valid.

COPING WITH THE EXPLODER: Put your hand up like a traffic cop and say, "Stop." Exploders often blow up because they feel threatened and yelling is their way of dealing with that emotion. Putting your hand up in this non-threatening way interrupts the tirade and will get the exploder speaking with you on an adult level. (Pointing your finger at them, on the other hand, could make them feel you're trying to challenge them.)

**EXPLODER** (shouting): I paid good money for this and it is nothing but a piece of —

**SALESPERSON** (holding his hand up like a traffic cop): Stop.

**"Stop!"**

**EXPLODER:** What?

**SALESPERSON:** I know you bought the camera. I know it's expensive. It's a good machine. Why isn't it working for you?

After the furor is over, give the exploder some time to compose himself. He will usually start listening and you can speak with him on an adult–adult level and focus on issues.

# Conclusion

Difficult people are a fact in business today as they have always been. Salespeople who avoid difficult people and the conflict they bring will be missing out on significant business opportunities: business that is easily accessible because most competing salespeople won't want to deal with those customers. Salespeople should remember that most difficult customers *can* be managed.

It is important that salespeople maintain a professional relationship by establishing credibility and asserting their own importance in the relationship. When salespeople encounter difficult customers, instead of getting drawn into situations that inevitably become lose–lose, they must start the coping behavior immediately.

If salespeople use the coping techniques with the Sherman tank, the super-agreeable, the know-it-all expert, and the exploder, then a win–win relationship will develop that will be rewarding professionally and financially for both the salesperson and the customer.

# Chapter 11
# FINANCIAL SELLING

Finances are also an important area of Personality Selling. If, however, you aren't usually involved in the finances of your customers, you may want to skip this chapter now and come back or refer to it only when needed.

## Personality Selling Gets Mathematical

Using financial concepts is especially important when selling to Sensing, Thinking, Intuitive, and Judging types. When these types of customers buy, they are using, whether they know it or not, financial techniques for making a decision. If you present information to them using financial concepts, your proposal is put in terms they understand and appreciate. Your buying cycle will often be reduced because financial selling provides such customers with all the information they need to make a decision to buy. When you structure your call using Personality Selling, the answer will almost always be "yes."

## Everybody Knows Finance

Many salespeople don't use financial concepts to sell, because finance has a reputation for being difficult to learn and apply. In reality, it is easy because everybody has and spends money.

Everybody knows finance. Every time you buy something, add to your savings, or invest in real estate because of the tax benefits, you are using financial techniques to manage your money.

When businesses decide to spend, save, invest, or reduce taxes they, too, are making financial decisions. Depending on what you sell, several categories of finance could be pertinent. For instance, if you sell capital equipment, like a new printing machine, there are several financial decisions to make. Are there cost-of-production savings? Should the project be financed out of savings? Are there depreciation and tax benefits?

The difference between the way a company makes financial decisions, as opposed to individuals, is that businesses make them more formally.

If you want to sell consultatively, you will need to help your customers finance your products. More important, knowing about finance will help you handle objections quickly and easily because you'll be able to structure proposals in terms your customer understands.

## Let Me Check the Budget

When your customers say they need to "check on the budget," they're going to decide financially. You need to understand what's going on so that you can help move the sales process forward and hold on to customers who are enthusiastic about your products.

You don't have to be a Wall Street wizard. All you have to do is speak intelligently about a few monetary concepts and understand the terminology to sell financially with success. The important concepts are the Time Value of Money, Net Present Value, Payback, and Replacement. Here's a look at how selling financially can help you. First, let's look at the time value of money.

## The Time Value of Money, or a Dollar Now Is Worth More Later

The Time Value of Money is the most "financial"-sounding term we'll look at, but it's the easiest to understand. All it means is that money will be worth more later than it is worth now. This is because of the interest money can earn. (If the interest rate someone gets on an investment is less than the inflation rate, then that money is actually worth less because it has less buying power at the end of the term.) How much more is the money worth? That depends. Think of the ways you can invest one thousand dollars. If you put it in a savings account, you could get five percent interest; if you put it in a moneymarket account, you could get eight percent; a bond might bring in ten percent, and investing in stocks could bring fifteen percent or more.

When you invest your money, you make a trade-off of how much you will eventually get versus the liquidity, or how easy it is to have your money available to you in cash.

This means that, if your customers put money in the bank, they can earn five to ten percent interest on their cash. If your product will save them or earn them more now than their bank will, it makes sense for them to buy your product instead of tying up their money in the bank.

> SALES REP: The copier I'm proposing costs one thousand dollars. If you put the same amount of money in a money-market account, in a year you'd make eighty dollars interest. Right?

**CUSTOMER:** Yes, that's about right.

**SALES REP:** You're spending five hundred dollars a year now having copies made at the printing shop. By buying the copier, that thousand dollars will bring you over four hundred dollars more in cost savings than putting it in the bank.

**CUSTOMER:** You're right.

# Net Present Value

The Net Present Value (NPV) is a financial method for figuring out how much money is worth when you figure in inflation and the interest it could earn. If there is no inflation, the NPV of $100 in a five percent savings account for a year is $105. The two are equal in financial value because $105 a year from now is worth $100 today. Calculators with business functions today have an NPV key that puts this selling detail at your fingertips.

## Most Salespeople Don't Use Net Present Value

Very few salespeople know what NPV is, and few use it in their presentations—much to their disadvantage. Presenting your products in terms of what money is worth now will add power and substance to your proposal for Sensing, Thinking, Intuitive, Judging, and Perceiving types because these types will want to know all the cost benefits of an item, present and future. Feeling types won't view NPV in itself as important, but will use it as valuable data in making their decision.

Thinking types will appreciate financial analysis the most because they like their decisions to be logical and analytical. NPV puts a buying decision in precisely those terms.

## Why Managers Always Use Net Present Value

The term Net Present Value became important in finances when inflation became a part of life. Managers know that inflation makes money worth less next year than it is this year. A manager on a budget gets a fixed sum to spend, and earns no interest. When he make budgets for projects that span five years or more, NPV is a way to figure out the cost of a long project in terms of the value of money today.

## Using Net Present Value Will Make *You* Money

If your customer intends to invest $100 per year for the next ten years, he would be better off financially having just $765 available to him today. A customer investing that amount would have $1,000 plus some interest in the bank, a total of about $1,258, *at the end of ten years.* According to NPV, that $765 today is worth $1,310 ten years from now.

> **SALESPERSON:** Instead of putting the money in the bank, why don't you use it to buy a new heater? The new heater will save you more money than you could have made in a savings account.

# Payback

The payback of a product is how long it will take for the product or service to justify its cost. If insulation costs one thousand dollars and you save five hundred a year in electricity costs, in two years you will have saved one thousand dollars—the same amount as originally spent. The payback, therefore, is two years.

## Two Years or Less Is a "Buy"

Most managers view products with paybacks of two years or less as too good to pass up, while paybacks of five years or more are "duds."

# Replacement

When people replace a product or a procedure, financial analysts assume it's because the new product or service saves money. Although that assumption is often too general, replacement analysis is based on the idea that people always want to save money.

## Cost of the Old vs. the New

When you do a replacement analysis, you figure out the cost of the way customers currently do things, and compare it to the cost of your proposed solution. You figure into the equation all the costs including depreciation, residual value, operating costs, repair costs, and any other additional or hidden costs you can find. You put the costs of both options side by side and see which comes up less.

## Replacement Analysis

Here's a replacement analysis for a company wishing to replace thirty typewriters with twenty computers. The replacement analysis is based on a computer life of five years. (State all figures in terms of Net Present Value if there are multi-year payments.)

| Documents Processing Annual Costs | Typewriters | Computers |
|---|---|---|
| Maintenance | $ 6,000 | $ 4,800 |
| Employees | $750,000 | $500,000 |
| Equipment | 0 | $ 20,000 |
| Depreciation | 0 | ($ 9,240) |
| Total Costs | $756,000 | $515,560 |
| Replacement savings of computers | | $240,440 |

MAINTENANCE: The computers are under warranty for the first year, while the typewriters are not under warranty and are expensive to fix.

EMPLOYEES: Since computers are faster and more efficient, twenty people using computers can do the same volume of work that it would take thirty people to do using typewriters. The annual salary of employees is $25,000 each.

EQUIPMENT: The typewriters are paid for, so cost nothing. The $100,000 total cost of the computers, spread over five years, amounts to an annual cost of $20,000.

DEPRECIATION: A tax deduction of $9,240 can be taken each of the first three years (assuming a 28% tax bracket). The typewriters have been fully depreciated and no more tax benefits are available.

TOTAL COSTS: These figures were reached by adding the cost of each set of equipment and its use and subtracting depreciation.

REPLACEMENT SAVINGS OF COMPUTERS: This is the difference between the total cost of the computers and the total cost of the typewriters.

# Conclusion

Use financial selling to show the total cost of purchases and contrast that figure against other alternatives. People of many different personality types use financial techniques for deciding what to purchase. Using Personality Selling's financial concepts with these types will lessen the buying cycle. If you want to know more about finance, there are many good books available on introductory finance that expand on the concepts of the time value of money, net present value, payback, and replacement.

# Chapter 12
# THE NEXT STEP—JUST START SELLING!

Now that you know about Personality Selling, you're ready to take this knowledge into your territory. You may have already discovered an interesting side effect of Personality Selling. You not only understand yourself and your customers better, but your boss, co-workers, friends, and family as well.

## How People Decide to Become Salespeople

Though you may not remember, it's very likely that you made your first sale at around the age of two, when you convinced your father that your mother allowed, in fact encouraged, cookie eating an hour before dinner. All the classic elements of selling were there—making a presentation, answering questions, trial closing, handling objections, and your first little-tyke closing line, "Can I?"

When your father said, "I guess it would be all right," your sales-toddler heart experienced the sweet exhilaration of a "sale." Somehow that cookie was all the sweeter because it was a victory cookie.

As you grew, you became a sales-youngster, negotiating and creating good deals in the school cafeteria.

True sales techniques didn't emerge until adolescence, when there was a lot more at stake than cookies—important things like using the car, coming home late, and getting extensions on book reports.

By adolescence, you found you would sell slightly differently to your mother, father, teachers, peers. You didn't know why, but knew that if you changed your approaches slightly, depending on whom you were trying to "sell," you'd have a better chance of success. You'd started using Personality Selling without knowing it.

The key to successful selling is taking your natural sales style, the kind you developed in high school and has since proven to work for you, and refining it to take in different sales situations and customer types—in other words, perfecting your own style through Personality Selling, the marriage of sales skills and psychology.

# Before Going into Battle

Before going into battle against competing salespeople, here's some additional armor for you to wear. Although sales is one of the highest-paying professions in the world, many salespeople are unhappy with the amount of money they make, striving for ever more. This leads to a phenomenon sales managers, who are mostly nurturant of their sales force, dread—sales burnout. When salespeople come to realize that true wealth isn't money, they're happier with their paychecks and their jobs, and can avoid rep burnout.

# Wealth Isn't Money

What salespeople are looking for is wealth, but wealth can't be found in paychecks. Wealth is found in one's capabilities, and money is only a by-product of those capabilities. I discovered this one day after reading Robert Allen's *Creating Wealth*,[30] where I was introduced to the idea of wealth being a mind set. I came home to find fire engines from several towns in the area in front of what was left of my condominium. Everything I owned had burned in the fire. I soon learned that the insurance we all had on the condominium was woefully inadequate. I ended up paying mortgage on a property that, literally, no longer existed. My family, friends, and the Red Cross helped with housing and expenses, but if wealth was money or assets, I didn't have any.

A few days later, while taking a walk, I saw a man sleeping on a park bench, trying to keep warm under the help-wanted section of a newspaper. If wealth were money, and he had $30 or so in his pocket, he would have been wealthier than I was. But, seeing the help-wanted section, it came to me that companies hiring programmers would need to have computers for them, and I sold computers. I ran to a stand and picked up a copy of that very same paper that had been covering the vagrant, and started making calls. I got over one million dollars in business that year.

Your greatest asset is *who you are*. Wealth isn't money, but people who are wealthy often have money. They have money because they believe in their capabilities and inspire others to believe in them, also.

# When the Only Luck You Have Is Bad

Professional athletes, who excel at their sport, go through slumps. There are periods in every professional's life when hitters can't hit, pitchers can't find the plate, and receivers can't catch. Salespeople are no different. Every good salesperson will go through periods when he or she just can't seem to sell anything to anyone. When that happens to you: 1) remember that wealth is what's in your head, not in your wallet; 2) reread this book (especially chapter 2—on finding prospects) and go back to the fundamentals of Personality Selling; 3) ask your sales manager for help; and 4) remember that it's only temporary; you'll be back.

## Burn the Midnight Oil

When Ted Williams was in a batting slump, he was the first to arrive at Fenway and the last to leave. Take a tip from Ted. Be at work before your boss, stay after he or she leaves, or do both. After a few days of hard work, ask your boss for help. I don't know of a sales manager in the world who hasn't been through a slump, too, and wouldn't be happy to help a rep who is trying. A sales adage says, "Sales is a numbers game. Make enough calls and you're bound to sell something." There's a lot to that old saying. Try selling to as many people as you can, and your hard work will pay off. You'll be back on track before you know it.

# Your Personality Is Right

A lot in the book has talked about customers' personalities and how to sell to them. Sales is an exciting, rewarding, and challenging job. It's sometimes frustrating, too, but you've got the right personality to make it both profitable and enjoyable.

Someday, when you are feeling down, think of the people you've helped by selling to them. Maybe end-users benefited from your products, or people who bought from you got a promotion because of the good work you do. Some people see sales as a big money grab, but stop occasionally and think of the good things you've done for people. I think you'll impress yourself.

# Take Advantage of Every Opportunity

The American economy is like an all-you-can-eat buffet. With Personality Selling you can sell until you're satiated. Too many reps starve to death inches from the food. You get results when you look for opportunities. The story below proves that point—it's about two sales reps:

> Two shoe salespeople went to a remote island in the Pacific. After touring the place, both salespeople called their managers.
>
> Sales rep A reported, "Boss, the trip is a bust. I've been all over the island and no one wears shoes. I'm taking the next plane home."

Sales rep B called and said, "Boss, this place is great. I've been all over. No one has any shoes! We're going to be rich."

When are salespeople like salesman A? When they give up too soon instead of trying to make situations work. They say things like, "XYZ Company wouldn't be interested in my product" or, "There aren't any accounts in that territory" or "Customers don't like salespeople calling them on Monday mornings or Friday afternoons." Think of how often you've been tempted to make similar remarks but overcame them to get the order using your creativity and energy.

Don't let the status quo or the path of least resistance keep you from being successful. Opportunities are everywhere. Look for them. Instead of wasting energy finding reasons why difficult situations won't work, use that energy to make them work.

## Turn Up Your Thermostat

Have you ever noticed that when you have a great month, several other great months follow? This happens because you're confident and "on." Unfortunately, many reps take time off after big sales, wasting their best sales time on the golf course. After you make big sales, go after those prospects that have been giving you trouble. You'll get them.

## Find a Few Challenges

Find a few tough customers and go after them. List five new accounts that you would love to have. Follow the steps in Personality Selling, and try to make one or all of them yours. I frequently get letters or phone calls from seminar attendees telling me about sales that they made that they had thought were impossible. Use Personality Selling, your observation skills, talent, and drive to find the prospects, contact them, learn about them, and close them.

Have some long-term and short-term goals, both professional and personal. The goals you set are, of course, up to you, depending on your personality. You can talk them over with friends, a colleague or your boss. Write them down on a piece of paper, or post them on the refrigerator. Make sure your goals are realistic and attainable, then develop a strategy for achieving them. Your hard work will pay off professionally when the accounts you've been dreaming of buy from you.

## The Next Step

Tennyson put it best. "Strive, Go Forth, and Conquer."

# Appendix A
# THE SALES PERSONALITY GUIDE

This Sales Personality Guide test will help you determine your own preference type. It is based on answers sales reps who had taken the Myers-Briggs Type Indicator gave during Sales and Negotiation Training Company seminars.

**DIRECTIONS:** Read each of these forty items and circle either answer A or B, depending on which response fits you best. There are no right, wrong, or better answers. You'll find the key to scoring at the end of the test.

1. **If someone asks you a question, do you usually:**
   A) reflect for a few moments, then respond.
   B) respond quickly.
2. **Which is the most convincing to you:**
   A) a presentation with a lot of facts.
   B) a presentation with a strong overview.
3. **When you make a decision, are you mostly swayed by:**
   A) how you are sure it will turn out.
   B) how you hope it will turn out.
4. **You tend to like days that are:**
   A) action-packed.
   B) leisurely.
5. **You like:**
   A) short meetings.
   B) long meetings.
6. **When learning a new concept, you think a lot of details first:**
   A) are essential to understanding.
   B) are overwhelming.
7. **If you are buying something for someone else, are you concerned:**
   A) that you are buying the right thing.
   B) that they will like it.
8. **When you make an important decision, do you usually:**
   A) set a deadline to decide.
   B) decide when you are comfortable.

9. **Would you rather have meetings:**
   A) with one person.
   B) with a group of people.
10. **When describing something, do you usually:**
    A) describe it factually.
    B) describe it conceptually.
11. **You like selling to customers who are:**
    A) fair.
    B) nice.
12. **When you buy expensive things, they are usually:**
    A) purchased on a whim.
    B) well thought out.
13. **If a customer wants you to get back to him, would you prefer:**
    A) writing a proposal and sending it to him.
    B) meeting with him and talking about it.
14. **If someone made a presentation to you that had spelling mistakes in it, would you:**
    A) view that negatively.
    B) probably not notice or be bothered by it.
15. **When you buy something, are you more concerned with:**
    A) its cost vs. benefits.
    B) how much people will like it.
16. **If you made a bad decision, would you feel:**
    A) it was the best decision at the time.
    B) like you were rushed.
17. **Do you prefer being with people who are:**
    A) somewhat quiet.
    B) talkative.
18. **Do you tend to:**
    A) notice little things.
    B) not notice little things.
19. **When you think about a new target market, do you tend to think of the demographic segment:**
    A) as a group.
    B) as individuals.
20. **If you're given a deadline for making a decision, and there's not enough time, would you:**
    A) make it anyway, with the data you've got.
    B) allow the deadline to slip until you have all the data.

21. **Would you rather have a:**
    A) desk in an open area.
    B) private office.
22. **Do you like buying things that are:**
    A) the latest and greatest.
    B) tried and true.
23. **If you're at a meeting and two salespeople are arguing, do you:**
    A) feel bad there isn't harmony.
    B) assume that interpersonal conflict is unavoidable.
24. **You've just decided on a big purchase. Are you most likely:**
    A) worried it wasn't the right thing to buy.
    B) relieved the decision is over.
25. **Do you find your most tiring days to be:**
    A) days when there are a lot of meetings.
    B) days when you are alone.
26. **Do you find untried, new ideas:**
    A) interesting and useful.
    B) sometimes interesting, but often unworkable.
27. **If your company has a price increase you know is going to be financially difficult for some customers, would you:**
    A) feel bad they'll be upset about the increase.
    B) assume that price increases are inevitable.
28. **If you overload your appointment schedule one day, would you:**
    A) try to reschedule some of the appointments.
    B) try to keep all the appointments, even if it is difficult.
29. **If there is a long period of silence during a conversation, is it your inclination to:**
    A) fill it in.
    B) use it to think.
30. **When you make a buying decision, would you most want to know:**
    A) how it would fit into future plans.
    B) how it would benefit you immediately.
31. **If a customer complained about the company, would you:**
    A) take it personally.
    B) not take it personally.
32. **When you're not at work, do you have a:**
    A) general sense of time.
    B) concrete sense of time.

33. **Would you prefer:**
    A) introducing yourself to someone.
    B) having someone introduce you.
34. **Would you be swayed more by how:**
    A) concepts relate to facts.
    B) facts relate to concepts.
35. **After trying to make a disgruntled customer happy, with no luck, would you:**
    A) keep trying until you do succeed.
    B) give up.
36. **Are you usually:**
    A) late.
    B) on time.
37. **When thinking over a new idea, do you prefer:**
    A) taking a walk someplace quiet, alone.
    B) talking it out with colleagues.
38. **When faced with a new problem with no predetermined rules and regulations, would you:**
    A) think of as many solutions to the problem as possible, despite other established company procedures.
    B) work within the rules established for other company programs, using accepted company procedures.
39. **Do you feel your best buying decisions were made:**
    A) rationally and precisely.
    B) emotionally.
40. **When you have several options, do you:**
    A) decide when you are comfortable that you have enough information.
    B) set up a deadline for making a final decision, and then work to get all the information by that deadline.

**SCORING:**
Introvert/Extrovert scale
Add the **A** answers for questions
1, 5, 9, 13, 17, 37
Add the **B** answers for questions
21, 25, 29, 33, 37

Put the Total here:_____ I/E

If the Total is 5 or more, you're most likely an **Introvert**; otherwise, you're most likely an **Extrovert**.

Sensing/Intuitive scale
Add the **A** answers for questions
2, 6, 10, 14, 18
Add the **B** answers for questions
22, 26, 30, 34, 38

Put the Total here:＿＿＿＿＿ S/N

If the Total is 5 or more, you're most likely a **Sensing** type; otherwise, you're most likely an **Intuitive** type.

Thinking/Feeling scale
Add the **A** answers for questions
3, 7, 11, 15, 19
Add the **B** answers for questions
23, 27, 31, 35, 39

Put the Total here:＿＿＿＿＿ T/F

If the Total is 5 or more, you're most likely a **Thinking** type; otherwise, you're most likely a **Feeling** type.

Judging/Perceiving scale
Add the **A** answers for questions
4, 8, 16, 20
Add the **B** answers for questions
12, 24, 28, 32, 36, 40

Put the Total here:＿＿＿＿＿ J/P

If the Total is 5 or more, you're most likely a **Judging** type; otherwise, you're most likely a **Perceiving** type.

NOTE: This is *not* the Myers-Briggs Type Indicator and it is not intended to be a substitute for the MBTI. This guide, designed to determine sales personality, is based on answers salespeople, who had previously taken the MBTI, gave to questions during Sales and Negotiation Training Company seminars.

# Appendix B
# A REVIEW OF THE SALES PROCESS

Here's a review of the steps involved in selling, from finding an account to negotiation and closing the sale. For more specific information, refer to chapters 2 through 6.

## Cold Contacting (Chapter 2)

**STEP 1: Find the prospects.** Go to the business section of your library to find as many leads as you can handle.

**STEP 2: Know what you sell.** Know the difference between function and benefit. Sell holes and not drills. Although the people buy a drill, what they need is the hole that it makes.

**STEP 3: Which cold-contact method works best for you?** The three main types of cold-contacting are in-person, telemarketing, and by letter. Use the first area of Personality Selling, the Introvert/Extrovert index to figure out the most promising cold-calling method. Generally, Introverts prefer being alone while they work, while Extroverts prefer being with other people. A prospective customer's preference on the Introvert/Extrovert index determines the best way to cold-contact him or her.

Use the listing of the types of profession Introverts and Extroverts gravitate towards in chapter 2 to get an idea of what type your prospects and customers are.

**STEP 4: Which cold-contact method is best for the customer?** Know the pluses and minuses of each method, as well as keys for successfully cold-calling each personality type.

**STEP 5: Start the meeting.** Find the best way to start the meeting and establish your objectives early.

**STEP 6: Show the customer you know your business and theirs.** Use your knowledge, experience, and empathy to win your customer's confidence.

**STEP 7: Gather information.** Listening is the key to a successful first meeting. Be an active listener.

**STEP 8: Find out what customers like and dislike about their current products and vendors.** Give them a reason to change by keeping the same whatever the customer likes about the current product or vendor, while changing as many things as you can that the customer doesn't like.

**STEP 9: Qualify the customer.** Qualifying is the process by which you can find out if the customer is ready, willing, and able to buy. Use the DARN-IT (Desire, Authority, Resources, Need, Interest, and Timing) test. Question prospects using non-threatening questions to get the qualifying information you need.

**STEP 10: Ask for an order or schedule another meeting** (if they're qualified). Don't leave the prospect hanging. Get a commitment from the customer. Commitments include orders, information, or a second meeting.

# The Presentation (Chapter 3)

**STEP 1: Have a pre-presentation meeting or conversation with at least one key member of the group.** This lets you test-market your pitch. It also helps develop a strategic partnership with a group member who'll be supportive during the meeting.

**STEP 2: Establish the goals of the meeting.**

**STEP 3: Find out if the group is Sensing, Intuitive, or a mix.** Discover the group's type to maximize the effectiveness of your presentation.

**STEP 4: Make the presentation.** Answer questions using the "feature–function–benefit–advantage" technique. This technique insures that customers will understand how and why each facet of your solution is something they should buy.

# Trial Close and Handling Objections (Chapter 4)

**STEP 1: Ask for questions.** See if there's any more information gathering to do.

**STEP 2: Begin the trial close.** The trial close is a query very early in the sales cycle asking the customer to buy. It sometimes elicits a sale, but its real function is to get a response or a reaction from the customer.

**STEP 3: Begin the assumptive close.** The assumptive close is a statement that assumes that the salesperson already has the order.

**STEP 4: Gauge their reaction.** If the customer's reaction is positive, move on to the next step. If the reaction is negative, go back to information gathering.

**STEP 5: Float the trial balloon.** The trial balloon is a closing question that is not designed to close the sale, but to get a reaction from the customer.

**STEP 6: Handling objections.** If the trial balloon doesn't elicit a positive response, then ask the customers to explain outstanding concerns. After you know their concerns, give your customers information that will eliminate the concerns or structure a win–win solution with them.

**STEP 7: Moving on.** If all the objections are handled and the customer has reacted positively to the trial balloon, the rep is ready to close the sale.

# Getting the Order (Chapter 5)

**STEP 1: Review the customer's buying criteria.** Review with the customer his criteria for making a decision.

**STEP 2: Ask if your solution fits the customer's buying criteria.**

**STEP 3: Ask for the order.**

**STEP 4: Write up the order or go back to objection handling.** Any complete sale often involves repeating steps. An attempted real close often brings out objections that the trial closes didn't bring out.

**STEP 5: Handle lingering objections,** if necessary. Lingering objections are small concerns the customer has that still keep him from placing an order. Tie up loose ends to get an agreement signed.

# Negotiation (Chapter 6)

**STEP 1: The customer asserts his position.**

**STEP 2: You bring information.**

**STEP 3: The customer asserts his other positions (if any).**

**STEP 4: You bring more information that would affect his opinion.**

**STEP 5:** Discover the issues—both yours and your customer's.

**STEP 6:** Develop a solution that will satisfy both parties.

| | Index 1 | Index 2 | Index 3 | Index 4 |
|---|---|---|---|---|
| Relates to: | **COLD CONTACT** | **HOW TO PRESENT** | **HANDLING OBJECTIONS** | **CLOSING THE SALE** |
| | INTROVERT | SENSING | THINKING | JUDGING |
| | EXTROVERT | INTUITIVE | FEELING | PERCEIVING |

# NOTES

1. Personality Selling is a registered trademark and servicemark of Sales and Negotiation Training Company.
2. Carl Jung, *Psychological Types* (New York: Harcourt Press, 1923).
3. The Myers-Briggs Type Indicator is a registered trademark of Consulting Psychologists Press, Inc. The MBTI is a trademark of Consulting Psychologists Press, Inc.
4. Thomas Moore, "Personality Tests Are Back," *Fortune* (March 1987), 74–82.
5. Isabel Briggs Myers and Mary H. McCaulley, *A Guide to the Use and Development of the Myers-Briggs Type Indicator* (Palo Alto, Calif.: Consulting Psychologists Press, 1985), 44.
6. Myers and McCaulley, *Guide to MBTI*, 244.
7. Myers and McCaulley, *Guide to MBTI*, 244–246.
8. David Keirsey and Marilyn Bates, *Please Understand Me: Character and Temperament Types* (Del Mar, Calif.: Promethcus Nemesis Books, 1978), 14.
9. Pamela L. Alreck and Robert B. Settle, *The Survey Research Handbook* (Homewood, Ill.: Richard Irwin, Inc., 1985), 45.
10. John Caples, *How to Make Your Advertising Make Money* (Englewood Cliffs, N.J.: Prentice-Hall, 1983), 141–147.
11. Caples, *Advertising Make Money* 141–147.
12. Thomas Peters and Nancy K. Austin, *A Passion for Excellence: The Leadership Difference* (New York: Random House, 1985), 72–75.
13. M. Scott Peck, *The Road Less Travelled* (New York: Touchstone Books, 1978), 120–131.
14. Irving Wallace, David Wallechinsky, and Amy Wallace, *The Book of Lists* (New York: Bantam Books, 1983), 469.
15. Myers and McCaulley, *Guide to MBTI*, 246–248.
16. Myers and McCaulley, *Guide to MBTI*, 248–250.
17. Myers and McCaulley, *Guide to MBTI*, 250–253.
18. Roger Fisher and William Ury, *Getting to Yes: Negotiating Agreement Without Giving In* (New York: Houghton Mifflin, 1981), 101.
19. Fisher and Ury, *Getting to Yes*.
20. T. Edward Damer, *Attacking Faulty Reasoning* (Belmont, Calif.: Wadsworth Pub., 1987).
21. Thomas Moore, "Personality Tests Are Back," *Fortune* (March 1987), 74–82.
22. Robert Bramson, *Coping with Difficult People* (New York: Dell, 1988), 14–25.
23. Robert Bramson, *Coping with Difficult People*.

24. Claude M. Steiner, *Scripts People Live* (New York: Bantam Books, 1975), 253–267.
25. Bramson, *Coping with Difficult People,* 4–5.
26. Eric Berne, *What Do You Say After You Say Hello?* (New York: Grove Press, 1973).
27. Berne, *After Hello?*
28. Bramson, *Coping with Difficult People,* 14–25.
29. Eric Berne, *Games People Play* (New York: Grove Press, 1964).
30. Robert Allen, *Creating Wealth* (New York: Simon & Schuster, Inc., 1983), 290.
31. Robert Benfari, *Understanding Your Management Style: Beyond the Myers-Briggs Indicator* (Lexington, Mass.: Lexington Books, 1991), 35–39.

# INDEX